INTERCESSION
Moving Mountains by
Living Eucharistically

INTERCESSION
Moving Mountains by
Living Eucharistically

By
Rev. George W. Kosicki, C.S.B.

Published by

Faith
Publishing Company
P.O. BOX 237
MILFORD, OHIO 45150

1996

Published by: Faith Publishing Company
                  P.O. Box 237
                  Milford OH 45150-0237
                  Phone: 513-576-6400
                  Fax: 513-576-0022

Bookstores or other book distributors may acquire additional copies of
this book by contacting Faith Publishing Company.

Individuals requesting additional copies of this book should contact:

                  The Riehle Foundation
                  P.O. Box 7
                  Milford OH 45150-0007
                  Phone: 513-576-0032

Published in the United States of America

ISBN: 1-880033-20-8

Library of Congress Catalog Card No.: 96-083752

Scriptural passages herein, except where noted, taken from the text of
the New American Bible, 1970, by the Confraternity of Christian
Doctrine.

Table of Contents

Dedication

To Mary, the Mother of Jesus Christ, the eternal High Priest, and my mother.

In thanksgiving to the Lord for Sister Gloria Beaupre, a Sister of the Society of St. Joseph, who died in West Hartford, CT in February, 1976, after she saw her life's wish fulfilled: to see a community of priests interceding for priests. She lived and died her motto: L. O. V. E.

Live
Our
Vocation
Eucharistically.

In thanksgiving to our "Bethany family," all the priests and associates of Bethany House of Intercession, who continue to intercede for the Shepherds of the Church.

Let us confidently approach the throne of grace to receive mercy and favor and find help in time of need (*Heb* 4:16).

Introduction

Origins

In this book we address the questions of intercession, of priesthood, and of Eucharist from a stance that is intended to increase faith, reverence, and commitment to Jesus Christ and to His Church.

All believers by their Baptism share in the three-fold office of Jesus Christ: Prophet, Priest, and King (Pastor). Here, we will consider the Priestly office of Jesus Christ. We share in that role both as the priesthood of the faithful, and as the ordained priesthood—the Priesthood of Christ that is exercised by bishops and priests through the sacrament of Holy Orders.

The role of the priesthood, specifically as ordained priests, is intercessory. But intercession is also the work of the whole royal priesthood—priests and faithful.

The main purpose of this book is to awaken in the whole Church—priests, religious and faithful—the need and urgency to intercede in this time of crisis in the Church and world. Our current situation calls for a sovereign action by God—our part is to intercede for mercy. Intercession is a right and duty that belongs to all of us.

We will be asking such questions as "What is intercession? What is its basis? How do we intercede? Why do we intercede? Who is to do the interceding?"

In the summer of 1974, Father Gerald Farrell, MM, missionary in Korea, shared his gift of intercessory prayer with our first *40 Days of Intercession for Priests*, held at St. John's Seminary in Plymouth, Michigan. Some one hundred priests joined the core group for part or all of the period of intercession. For the next nine years, this gift of intercessory prayer was the foundation of our ministry to some 2,000 priests from around the world, as the core group (12 in all) carried on a daily program of interceding for priests.

Over some nine years we have written about our experiences of intercession. After our first program of intercession in 1974 we described what we did in the booklet *Forty Days of Intercession for Priests* (Word of Life, 1975, Ann Arbor, MI 48107). After four years in Bethany House of Intercession, located at Our Lady of Providence Seminary, Warwick, RI, we described our experience with hundreds of priests in *Intercessory Prayer: Rediscovering the Priestly Dimension.* This pamphlet, now out of print, was addressed to priests, drawing examples from Bethany House of Intercession. In the same year we addressed religious sisters on the subject of intercession in *Intercession: The Power to Renew, Sisters Today.*

This present work focuses on the Eucharist and is addressed to all the faithful, to all the royal priesthood. This priestly dimension of our intercession is based on our baptism. So by our baptism we are all intercessors; we are *all* a royal priesthood, offering the Immaculate Victim and ourselves in the Eucharist for the salvation of the whole world.

In the light of the Second Vatican Council teaching on the Eucharist it can be said that, "the ultimate truth of the Catholic Church is the Eucharist." To me this means that the Word of God became flesh and dwells among us. This also means that the Word of God did not become just a book by which we live—but rather more than that—the Word of God became Eucharist in order that *we* become the bread of life, to offer a continual sacrifice of praise for the salvation of the world to the glory of the Father. This also means that we become this bread in the way Jesus did—by the power of the Holy Spirit in the womb of Mary.

Overview

Jesus is our priest who lives forever to make intercession for us. (see *Heb* 7:22-35). Jesus, as priest, is interceding for us now. This has been his role at the throne of the Father for these twenty centuries. Moreover, it is Jesus who has called us, the members of His Body, to participate also in this priestly work of intercession. It is the source of our dignity as a royal priesthood.

We *are* a royal priesthood—we *are* intercessors with and in Him Who is the one mediator before the Father. Sharing in his priesthood is not only a calling, it is also a duty. Because He has chosen and sanctified us, He wants us to cooperate with Him in His work of bringing salvation to all who approach God through Him (see *Heb* 7:25 and 9:28). We have a duty to be intercessors with Him before the Father and so to be channels of His mercy to all.

In practice this means we are to be priests—always and everywhere offering a sacrifice of thanks and praise, offering our whole created beings, that is our bodies, as a living sacrifice holy and acceptable to God. It means that we are to be imitators of Christ who gave Himself for us out of love as an offering to God (see *Eph* 5:1 and *Jn* 3:16) for all who believe.

Intercession is a *priestly* action. Both the priestly people and ordained priests are priests because we share in Christ's priesthood, each of us in a unique way.

And it is by our *Baptism* that we are this priestly people, this royal priesthood. This is the teaching of the Church as expressed in the Second Vatican Council:

> The baptized, by regeneration and the anointing of the Holy Spirit, are consecrated to be a spiritual house and a holy priesthood, that through all the works of Christian men they may offer spiritual sacrifices and proclaim the perfection of Him who called them out of darkness into His marvelous light (cf. *1 Pet* 2:4-10) (*Lumen Gentium,* 10).

All baptized believers share in the one priesthood of Christ. However, some are *ordained* for a special role of service and sacrifice. Again the Second Vatican Council is clear:

> However, the Lord also appointed certain men as ministers, in order that they might be united in one body in which "all the members have not the same function" (*Rom* 12:4) (*Presbyterorum Ordinis,* 2).

And in the document on the Church:

Though they differ essentially and not only in degree, the common priesthood of the faithful and the ministerial or hierarchical priesthood are none the less ordered one to another; each in its own proper way shares in the one priesthood of Christ (*Lumen Gentium*, 10).

Through the sacrament of Holy Orders, Christ so configures bishops and priests to Himself that, when they pronounce the words of consecration they act "in the person of Christ, since the celebrant, by reason of this special sacrament, identifies himself with the Eternal High Priest, Who is both author and principal agent of His own sacrifice in which truly no one can take His place" (John Paul II, *Dominicae Cenae*, 1980).

This is an overview in sweeping lines—a panorama of what Christ Jesus did and is doing and of what we are to do now to be imitators and disciples—apostles—brothers and sisters of Him Who is our eternal High Priest.

The purpose of this book is to flesh out the meaning, the duty, and the practice of being intercessors. We will come to see that there are different kinds of intercession and different times and places for intercession, but we will also come to see that all intercession converges at the cross of Our Lord Jesus Christ, which is made present to us *now* in His Holy Eucharist.

To be an intercessor is to be one in Christ—one priest, one victim, one body, through the one Spirit to the glory of God, the Father, for the salvation of the world.

To be an intercessor is to be a living Eucharist crying out: "Father, behold Your Son! and have mercy on us and on the whole world."

Rev. George W. Kosicki, C.S.B.

Chapter 1

The Need for Intercession *NOW*

As I and many others look at the world in its present situation, various indicators point to a time of great difficulty ahead. This present age is on a collision course politically, economically, socially, ecologically, and spiritually. There is no doubt that the world and the Church need help. We need to intercede, and we need to intercede *now.*

I believe that the times are so urgent and the needs of the Church are so great that no renewal program is adequate to the .situation. Only a sovereign act of God can save us. Only the mercy of God is our hope and salvation. These statements may sound dramatic or even desperate, but I believe they are a realistic appraisal of the situation. They are also a rewording of the exhortations of Pope Paul VI and Pope John Paul II to *"Implore the Spirit."* The Lord is bringing the Church and the world to its knees that we may repent and cry for His mercy.

We need to intercede for God's mercy *now*—in this time of travail.

This time of travail can bring forth life but it can also bring about death. If the Spirit of God hovers over the chaos, then new life comes forth. For this reason we must implore the Spirit to hover over our chaos and praise Him for His providential purification. We need the Spirit to bring us to the fullness of new life. To obtain the Spirit, we need only to ask for It, to implore the Spirit. This sounds like a simple solution, and in fact, it is. But it is also a simple and awesome fact that we can choose to refuse the Holy Spirit.

The basic response of the Church to this time of travail is to acknowledge that the Church is in fact in travail. The Lord is calling us, both priests and people, to stand together as Church at

1

the cross of Jesus, with Mary, in docility to the Father, crying, "I am a sinner. I repent. Forgive me. Mercy!" Together, united in mind and heart, we need to call out to the nations, "Come to the fount of mercy and bathe in it."

The response to the travail is to be fully priests—to offer ourselves, our sufferings and those of the whole world in union with Christ our eternal High Priest and Immaculate Victim for the salvation of the world. This is what it means to be a priestly people, a Eucharistic people, to be intercessors. This is to be as Eucharist. This is what it means to respond to the call to take up the cross. This call to stand at the cross is actually a call to martyrdom. How do I prepare for this martyrdom? By dying daily. By living in docility. By daily walking in the light in simple faith as a child, as a son, and by observing this exhortation:

> *Rejoice always, never cease praying, render constant thanks; such is God's will for you in Christ Jesus (1 Thes* 5:16-18).

It is a daily dying to live out the tension of rejoicing always at the Eucharist Table in hope, praying without ceasing while seated at the Throne of intercession. It is a daily dying to walk in the light—not in the dark and not even in twilight. Each of us knows what light and darkness are in our own lives and we know too, all too well, what the twilight is, the grey area in between. To walk in the light is to stand at the cross. To walk as a child, hand in hand with Jesus and Mary in docility, is to die daily to our pride and rebellious independence. This is to prepare for martyrdom.

And martyrdom is the preparation for the new Pentecost. The Church needs to continue to pray the prophetic prayer of Pope John XXIII so that every part of it may be fulfilled:

> Divine Spirit, renew Your wonders in this our age as in a new Pentecost, and grant that Your Church, praying perseveringly and insistently with one heart and mind together with Mary, the Mother of Jesus, and guided by Blessed Peter, may bring to fulfillment the reign of the Divine Savior, a reign of truth and justice, a reign of love and peace. Amen.

The new Pentecost is the preparation for the new Advent. It is my fervent hope and prayer that the Church will follow the lead of Pope John Paul II, united in the prayer with which he concluded his first encyclical:

> I implore Mary, the heavenly Mother of the Church, to be so good as to devote herself to this prayer of humanity's new Advent (*Redemptor Hominis,* 22).

Pope John Paul entitled the concluding chapter of his encyclical on mercy, "The Prayer of the Church in our Times." He wrote clearly and strongly for the need to intercede for mercy—now in this our critical times:

> . . . At no time and in no historical period—especially at a moment as critical as our own—can the Church forget *the prayer that is a cry for the mercy* of God amid the many forms of evil which weigh upon humanity and threaten it. . . .

> Modern man feels these threats. Modern man often anxiously wonders about the solution to the terrible tensions which have built up in the world and which entangle humanity. And if at times he lacks the courage to utter the word "mercy," or if in his conscience, empty of religious content, he does not find the equivalent, *so much the greater is the need for the Church to utter this word,* not only in her own name but also in the name of all the men and women of our time.

> Everything that I said in the present document on mercy should therefore be continually transformed into an ardent prayer: into a cry that *implores* mercy according to the needs of man in the modern world. . . . Let us have recourse to God through Christ, mindful of the words of Mary's *Magnificat,* which proclaim mercy "from generation to generation." Let us implore God's mercy for the present generation" (*Dives in Misericordia,* 15, emphasis in the text).

The time for intercession is NOW!

In a general audience address on June 1, 1983, Pope John Paul II gave a strong Eucharistic response to the exploding situation in the world and the need to intercede now. In part, he stated:

> Entering into the sacrificial offering of the Savior, the faithful participate in the victory which He won over the evil of the world. When we are shaken by the vision of evil which is widespread in the universe, with all the devastations it produces, we should not forget that the unleashing force of sin is curbed by the saving power of Christ. Every time that the words of consecration are pronounced in the Mass and the Body and Blood of the Lord are made present in the act of sacrifice, there is also present the triumph of love over hatred, of holiness over sin. Every Eucharistic celebration is more powerful than all the evil of the universe; it signifies a real, concrete fulfillment of the Redemption and an ever deeper reconciliation of sinful humanity with God in the perspective of a better world (*L'Osservatore Romano,* June 6, 1983).

Now is the time to cry for mercy for the Church and world. Now is the time to continually offer the sacrifice of "incarnate mercy" for us and for the whole world. Now is the time to intercede as a royal priesthood, as a priestly people, pleading for the salvation of the world.

Note: This chapter is based in part on material drawn from an earlier reflection on the situation in the Church and world: *Pilgrimage and Purification: the Church in Travail in the 80's,* G. W. Kosicki; Crux, 1980, Albany, NY 12204.

Chapter 2

An Intercessor is United with Christ Jesus

In his first epistle, St. Peter tells us that every Christian is, through the grace of baptism, a priest (see *1 Pet* 2:9). We exercise this priesthood in a number of ways, but none is more significant than participating in the priestly work of intercession . . . in praying for people, the Church, the world.

Jesus, our Chief Priest, is at this very moment interceding for us at the right hand of the Father. He has been doing this for almost 2,000 years. As Christians, priests united with the Chief Priest Himself, we are called to be intercessors with Him before the Father. And this intercession is not an optional part of Christian life. It is our duty because Jesus has chosen us and sanctified us. He wants us to cooperate with Him in His work of bringing salvation to all who approach God through Him. It is our duty as Christians to pray for the needs of the Body of Christ, to intercede with Jesus before the Father, and so to be channels of God's mercy.

In practice this means that we are to be active "priests," always and everywhere offering sacrifices of thanks and praise. It means that we are to offer our bodies as living sacrifices. It means that we are to be imitators of Christ, Who gave Himself as an offering for all who believe.

To be an intercessor is to be united with Christ: one priest, one victim, one body. We are united with Him through the one Spirit, to the glory of God the Father, for the salvation of the world.

What is Intercession?

The dictionary defines *intercede* as "to act between parties with a view to reconciling differences; to beg or plead on behalf of another; to mediate."

Jesus intercedes for us continuously. He pleads our cause before the Father's throne. He continues to mediate that we might be reconciled with God the Father, and toward this same end, we unite with Jesus' intercession by praying for people we know. We ask God to have mercy on them, to forgive them, to pour out His Spirit on them, to bless them, to give them the things they need in life. When we intercede we remind God of His promises to shower mercy and love upon His creatures.

We can find many examples of intercession in Scripture. For example, Moses was a constant intercessor, turning to the Lord again and again to ask mercy for His people:

> *But Moses implored the Lord his God saying, "Why, O Lord, should Your wrath blaze up against Your own people? . . . Let Your blazing wrath die down; relent in punishing Your people. Remember Your servants Abraham, Isaac, and Israel, and how You swore to them by Your own self. . . ." So the Lord relented in the punishment He had threatened to inflict on His people* (*Exod* 32:11-14).

This passage shows the three dimensions of intercession: action, prayer, and offering. Moses took action, standing between a sinful people and their angry God. He prayed that God would remember His promises to the people and not inflict the punishment He had threatened. And He offered Himself as a living sacrifice by being ready to do whatever God commanded as a result of His intercession.

Jesus is an intercessor in the same way. He became one of us, took on our sins and wounds, and laid down His life for us. He stood between an offended God and all of sinful humanity. He prayed that God would have mercy on all who would believe. And He went to the cross as an offering pleasing to the Father. His action, His prayer, and His offering won salvation for all.

Now we Christians are called, consecrated, and commissioned as intercessors in and with Christ Jesus. We act, pray, and offer intercession in union with Christ for the salvation of the world. (For recent official Church teaching on intercession see Appendix II, *Church Statements on Intercession*.)

Who is an Intercessor?

Many Christians today tend to look on intercession as a task for professionals—pastors, leaders, and those in cloisters. These "specialists," some people may think, intercede for the salvation of the world, and lay people need only ask for their daily needs. This is not true. When Jesus taught His disciples to pray and to take up their cross daily it was a lesson for all Christians. He wants us all to follow in His footsteps and to pray and offer sacrifices for others.

Paul teaches this same lesson throughout his epistles: Pray constantly, and bear your share of the hardships for the sake of the gospel. He gives us his own example of prayer and sacrifice as a model. For example, *"Ever since we heard this [news of your growth in Christ] we have been praying for you unceasingly and asking that you may attain full knowledge of His will through perfect wisdom and spiritual insight"* (*Col* 1:9). Paul also tells of his sacrifice: *"Even now I find my joy in the sufferings of Christ for the sake of His body, the church"* (*Col* 1:24).

As members of the Body of Christ we all have an obligation to pray for one another in the same way Paul did. No one is excused from this obligation. The old, the young, mothers, fathers, workers, students, the sick, the overburdened, the poor and the rich—all are called to intercede with Christ.

Why Intercede?

There are many good reasons for Christians to intercede. The most important is that we are told to do so by Jesus. It is stated throughout the Gospels, such as:

> *Ask the harvest-master to send laborers to His harvest* (*Lk* 10:2).

> *So I say to you, Ask and you shall receive, seek and you shall find, knock and it shall be opened to you* (*Lk* 11:9).

> *Until now you have not asked for anything in My name. Ask and you shall receive, that your joy may be full* (*Jn* 16:24).

Jesus tells us to intercede because it is the way we cooperate with Him to bring mercy, grace, and blessings to men and women on earth. In asking we are exercising our free will. We unite our will with His so that His will may be done. God wants us to ask Him for what we need and to intercede for all people, especially for those whom we know. As we do, we show reverence for God's will for humanity.

What do We Intercede For?

There is a need to know precisely what to intercede for so that we can all the more effectively focus our intercession toward that goal. To put it succinctly, we intercede for the outpouring of the Holy Spirit, for the Kingdom of God, for mercy, and for the Church.

We intercede first of all that the Spirit of the living God will come and live within us, the Christian people, so that the earth can be renewed. It is a plea for the continual outpouring of the Holy Spirit on believers and for successful evangelism of unbelievers. We are sent by the Spirit to evangelize, and to do this we must prepare the way by intercession.

We also intercede for the coming of Christ's kingdom. Where the Spirit of God is, there is the kingdom; there Jesus reigns to the glory of the Father. When we pray, "Father, Your kingdom come," we are interceding for the reign of Jesus as Lord. The Spirit prepares us for that reign of Jesus by converting our hearts and enabling us to experience the future kingdom in the present. The extent to which we receive and submit to the Holy Spirit is the extent to which the kingdom has come in our lives.

We also intercede for mercy—for God's love to pour into our hearts through the Holy Spirit. When we intercede for mercy, begging the Lord to "look not on our sins but on the faith of the Church," we are in perfect harmony with God's own plan for the salvation of the world. For He desires to have mercy on all.

We should also intercede for the Church. Our prayer should be that the Holy Spirit will possess the Church more and more, that the kingdom will come to its fulfillment in every member of the Church, that God's mercy will fill all in the Church to overflowing. The goal we should have in mind as we intercede for the Church is that it will actually become what God wants it to be—a Body of men and women fully in union with Him.

How to Intercede

There are various ways to intercede. We can do it sponta-neously; we can use the prayers found in scripture, especially the psalms and the prayers of the apostles in the first several chapters of the Acts of the Apostles; or we can turn to traditional prayers like the Lord's Prayer and the Rosary. All are very effective, practical ways to intercede for God's will to be done on earth. However, it is not just prayer alone.

Intercession should be backed up with self-denial. Fasting is a particularly effective way to add heart to our intercession.

For Catholics intercession is related to the Eucharist, which is Jesus present to us. We can extend the power of the Eucharist to each moment of the day as we pray with praise and thanksgiving for the needs of God's people.

Much more can and should be said about intercession. But the point I want to leave you with, my brothers and sisters, is that every one of us is able and obligated to intercede every day for the people of God.

Chapter 3

Mary, the Model of Intercession

If we want to see the goal of our intercession already fulfilled, the Church has taught us to look to Mary, the Mother of God. The documents of Vatican II state:

> Through the gift and role of divine maternity, Mary is united with her Son, the Redeemer, and with His singular graces and offices. By these the Blessed Virgin is also united with the Church (*Lumen Gentium*, 63).

> In the most Holy Virgin the Church has already reached that perfection whereby she exists without spot or wrinkle (*ibid.,* 65).

In Mary, the Church has already reached perfect union! Mary is God's perfect creation—chosen, Immaculate Daughter of the Father, Spouse of the Spirit and Mother of the Son. God wanted to give us a perfect being and He did so in creating Mary. Now He wants us to seek this same perfection. All the graces and roles Mary has received are for us, the Church, His Body.

So we intercede that the Church becomes like Mary, its perfect model—that we become holy like our heavenly Father is holy. Thus we fulfill the command of Jesus to be holy (see *Mt* 5:48; 6:33) and fulfill the command of Jesus to take Mary as our own (see *Jn* 19:25-27). The Second Vatican Council put it this way: "Seeking after the glory of Christ, the Church becomes more like her exalted model (Mary), and continually progresses in faith, hope, and charity, searching out and doing God's will in all things" (*Lumen Gentium*, 65).

Mary, Mother of Mercy and Spouse of the Spirit, Pray for Us

When we intercede for the coming of the Spirit, the coming of the kingdom, for mercy, and for the holiness and unity of the Church, we are praying for a new Pentecost. This reign of Jesus in our hearts and this time of special mercy (a new advent, according to John Paul II), all of this is praying for a sovereign action of God. It also becomes the triumph of the Immaculate Heart of Mary.

As we have already mentioned, what God has in mind for us is already fully and perfectly accomplished in Mary. She, who by God's design and choice is sinless and totally submissive to God's Spirit and will, shares in the triumph of the reign of Jesus and intercedes for us. She intercedes that the triumph she shares will also be ours. So we pray to her to intercede for us sinners:

Holy Mary, Mother of God, pray for us sinners now and at the hour of our death.

Mary, as you formed Jesus by the power of the Holy Spirit, form us by the same Holy Spirit into the one Body of your Son.

Mary, since you are spouse of the Spirit and mother of mercy teach us to yield to the Spirit that we may be channels of mercy to the world.

Lord, fill us with Your Spirit, possess us that Your Spirit can use us for the fulfillment of Your kingdom as it is fulfilled in Mary our Queen.

Lord, fill us with Your Holy Spirit, that we may be holy as the Father is holy, and immaculate as Mary Your mother is Immaculate.

Lord, fill us with Your mercy so that we may be over-flowing vessels of Your mercy like Mary, our Mother of Mercy.

Chapter 4

Principles of Intercession

There are various ways to intercede and they are all related to the Eucharist. Here we will look at some principles that can extend the Eucharist to each moment of the day as we pray with praise and thanks for the needs of the Church. These principles reflect my own experience of intercession as a priest in the community at Bethany House of Intercession. These principles, however, also apply to the intercession of the royal priesthood as we live Eucharistically.

Repent of Self-Concern

"Repent of self-concern and be concerned for the Church and the kingdom" is a word that we received in prayer as a theme of our intercession. We asked the priests who came to intercede in prayer with us to set aside their personal burdens for at least three days. In a sense, we asked them to take off that personal knapsack full of self-concern and leave it at the door during their stay at Bethany. We asked them to concentrate on interceding for brother priests whom they know personally and for priests who are experiencing the same or even worse burdens. To our delight we have found this really works. Hundreds of priests have tried it and when they returned to their knapsack, they found the Lord had taken care of their personal needs in His special way. We called this the *three-day resurrection principle,* recalling the three days of Jesus in the tomb before the Father raised Him to glory.

Priests tend to be introspective when they are burdened and their introspection hinders the healing the Lord would like to give them. Taking the focus off of ourselves gives the Lord a chance to work in His way.

This principle is a fundamental one that sets the tone and attitude of intercession for the whole of the royal priesthood, ordained and laity alike: be concerned for the needs of others rather than your own.

Two-Fold Healing

From our experience, we found that many priests are in search of personal healing. I think that many of them do not actually need personal healing so much as they need intercession! The burdens they carry are not just their own, but also the burdens of their people. What is really needed is a two-fold healing: the people's and their own. As priests intercede for the people's need, they will experience that two-fold healing. Their intercession will lift the burden from the lives of their people and at the same time, lift away their own burdens. It is a very basic principle that arises from their ordination as victim-intercessors.

In a similar way many of the faithful seek personal healing for their own burdens. But, in fact, they are also experiencing the burdens of others—the burdens are not just their own. The response to victimhood (to the burden) is not to be overwhelmed but rather to intercede and seek a two-fold healing, that is, the healing of those in need as well as our own.

Perhaps there is an important question that needs to be asked here about healing:

How healed do I need to be in order to be an intercessor? How much healing do I need to receive before I can embrace the cross of Christ for others?

I would venture to say that an intercessor needs to be healed enough to embrace the cross with peace and joy. Peace and joy come as a gift of the Holy Spirit and are the measure of the healing we need to intercede with Christ.

But in the midst of suffering the burden, we are usually in no position to analyze and distinguish all its various roots and causes because the present suffering overshadows our discernment. One response we can always make, however, is to ask for the Holy Spirit to come and overshadow the chaos and bring forth new life. Hovering over the chaos is the Holy Spirit's specialty (see *Gen* 1:2).

The most effective intercession for the coming of the Holy Spirit is in the Eucharist. Here, the Spirit transforms bread and wine into the Body and Blood of Christ. Here, the Spirit is invoked to transform us with our burdens into the broken Body of Christ Who is pleading for mercy and the ultimate healing for us—eternal healing—eternal salvation.

Interceding at the Intersections

The word *intercession* in both the Greek and Hebrew has as one of its root meanings, "to chance upon." This meaning of the word has foundation in our experiences. I call it *interceding at the intersection.* As we experience different events and people coming to mind, as though by chance, we intercede further. God in His providence has probably placed this situation before us so that we might join His intentions in doing something about it. In other words, the intersection of our lives and someone else's has been planned by God for a purpose, namely, that we might intercede for that person. The awareness of another's needs is a discernment given us, not that we judge and criticize, but that we intercede with thanks and praise.

Each and every need that comes to our minds and weighs upon our hearts we can offer in union with the Eucharistic Lord.

Interceding with Thanks and Praise

St. Paul exhorts us *"to render constant thanks"* (*1 Thes* 5:17), *"to dedicate yourselves to thankfulness"* (*Col* 3:15), *"and to pray in a spirit of thanksgiving"* (*Col* 4:2). As we intercede for others the main pattern our prayer often takes is one of thanks and praise to the Lord. Since we are striving to listen to the Lord for His desires and to pray according to His will, then our intercessions are offered with thanks and praise because we know that He is already answering our prayer.

Strive "to render constant thanks" or as other translations put it, "to give thanks in all circumstances." Thus we are striving to give constant thanks *in* all circumstances. This is an important distinction from giving thanks *for* all circumstances. The point is that we can always thank God because He is Lord and God of *all* circumstances. We do not thank Him for the evil; rather we thank Him that He makes all things turn out for the good of those who love Him (see *Rom* 8:28). God does not directly will the evil but He allows it for the good to be accomplished in His great and marvelous plan. So in every circumstance the Lord wants us to give thanks and not allow sin or evil to dampen our thanks and praise. In every situation the Lord is present; He is in charge; He is Lord.

Living a life of constant thanks is living a Eucharistic life.

Binding and Unbinding (Bless, do not Curse)

We have a great power to curse and to bless, but most of us are unaware of this power. By our resentments, anger, criticism or negative feelings toward another, for example our Bishop, we in effect curse him and keep him bound—and ourselves as well.

For example, to bring reconciliation to a brother and ourselves, we can intercede for him. We can do this by forgiving his wrongs and sins, by unbinding him from our resentments and negative feelings, by asking the Lord to cut these bindings and heal them, and by blessing him, asking the Lord to pour down upon him His love, His Holy Spirit and renew his life.

The power to bind and to loose (see *Mt* 16:19 and 18:18) accompanies the keys that are entrusted to the Church. Not only can we unlock, but unwittingly we can lock up and bind and not realize we are responsible. By our forgiveness, unbinding, and blessing, we can even bring freedom to people at a distance. We can broadcast forgiveness and love to those who need it. Jesus put it this way:

> *Love your enemies, do good to those who hate you; bless those who curse you and pray for those who maltreat you (Lk 6:27-28).*

And St. Peter put it this way:

> *Do not return evil for evil or insult for insult. Return a blessing instead. This you have been called to do, that you may receive a blessing as your inheritance (1 Pet 3:9).*

We can bring a lot of freedom to many if we learn to bless, rather than curse. To bless is to live Eucharistically. To bless in the Eucharist is the greatest blessing. We must learn to intercede "in behalf of," not "in spite of."

Taking Spiritual Authority

Our sin gives the devil that foothold in our lives. But fortunately, we have been given authority over Satan and his forces and can cast them off. Our experience at Bethany House of

Intercession has shown us that interceding involves resisting the work of the Evil One. For us it is living out *The Our Father* and daily putting on the spiritual armor (see *Eph* 6:10-20). After our Morning Prayer, the prayer leader of the day would lead us in taking spiritual authority over any spirits of darkness that might interfere with our lives or those of priests we were praying for. He might pray this way:

> In the name of Jesus and by His Precious Blood, I take authority over you, Satan, and your evil spirits at work in us and bind you to Jesus and order you to be gone.

We have found that taking spiritual authority is necessary in our intercession and also effective as St. Peter taught us:

> *Resist him, solid in your faith, realizing that the brotherhood of believers is undergoing the same sufferings throughout the world (1 Pet 5:9).*

The ministry of intercession is a ministry of establishing the Kingdom of God where it does not exist as well as protecting those who are in the kingdom. Union with our Eucharistic Lord gives us a share in His victory and His authority. For He has told us:

> *. . . the Prince of this world is at hand. He has no hold on Me (Jn 14:30).*

Unity in Interceding

Unity of heart and mind of those interceding is a fundamental principle. To be effective in our prayer we need to agree and "join our voices" as well as our hearts in what we ask of the Father. The agreeing is the hardest part.

> *If two of you join your voices [agree] on earth to pray for anything whatever, it shall be granted you by my Father in heaven (Mt 18:19).*

During communal intercessory time we need to set aside our own intentions for the moment and submit to the intentions being presented. But more fundamentally, our unity must be one of love for one another with no obstacles or sin between us. Our experience is that the effectiveness of our ministry is in direct proportion to our love for one another.

It is this kind of unity that the Lord Jesus prayed for (see *Jn* 17) so that the world would believe and know that He was sent from the Father.

Our experience at Bethany House has also shown us that as we come to greater unity of heart and mind in Christ, we become isolated from values of the world that are not of Christ. To the extent that we are united to Christ in more and more areas, to that extent we take a prophetic stance. Such a united stance can mean being criticized and rejected by those who are not of the same heart and mind.

For the strength and courage to intercede in this united way— this prophetic way—we need the strength that comes from being nourished by the sacrament of unity, the Eucharist. St. Paul taught clearly that we need a basic unity to celebrate the Sacrament of unity effectively (see *1 Cor* 11:17-34).

The Spirit Interceding in our Hearts

The Holy Spirit is continually interceding in our hearts. To intercede, then, is to unite ourselves with the intercession already going on. It is like tuning in the same channel on which the Holy Spirit is broadcasting. To intercede then is not so much what I do, as what I allow to go on in and through me as I unite myself with the Spirit interceding in my heart. St. Paul wrote of this intercession in the context of all creation groaning.

> *The Spirit too helps us in our weakness, for we do not know how to pray as we ought; but the Spirit Himself makes intercession for us with groanings that cannot be expressed in speech. He Who searches hearts knows what the Spirit means, for the Spirit intercedes for the saints as God Himself wills (Rom 8:26-27).*

The term, "groanings in our hearts," is a way of describing praying in tongues. Because we do not know how to intercede for so many needs, sometimes we pray more freely in tongues, praying in the Spirit, using all prayer and supplication and inspired songs (see *Eph* 5:19-20; 6:18-19). We find this gift a great blessing that enables us to thank and praise the Lord. A very practical aspect of praying in tongues is, "that we do not tire out our head trying to make up all the prayers that would be needed," nor do we try to control the nature or direction of prayer for each situation.

Another way of interceding in the Spirit is to "hold the other person in your heart." It is a way of uniting ourselves with others by a loving desire that the Lord's will be fulfilled in their lives as the Lord reveals His love to them. It is a way of allowing the Spirit in our hearts to embrace them with love. It is a way of lifting them up to the Lord.

In the great intercession of the Church—the Eucharist—the Spirit unites us with the intercession of our Lord Jesus at the throne of the Father.

Interceding in the Name of Jesus

I give you my assurance, whatever you ask the Father, He will give you in my name. Until now you have not asked for anything in my name. Ask and you shall receive that your joy may be full (Jn 16:23-24).

To ask in the name of Jesus means to ask in union with the person of Jesus. And so *"where two or three are gathered in my name, there am I in their midst" (Mt 18:20).* When we intercede in the name of Jesus, we intercede *with* Jesus and *not against* Him, as though He were on the opposite team and we needed to plead and bargain with Him. To intercede in the name of Jesus, we unite ourselves with His will, His desires, and pray with Him as we approach the Father. So the needs we ask for are not so much for our own self-satisfaction, but rather, for the needs of the Church and kingdom as best we know them.

When we intercede in the name of Jesus,

We have this confidence in God; that He hears us whenever we ask for anything according to His will. And since we know that He hears us whenever we ask, we know that what we have asked Him for is ours (1 Jn 5:14-15).

Interceding in the Name of Jesus is most fully expressed in the Eucharist where the priest acts in the very Person of Jesus, using the very words of Jesus and says, ". . . this is My Body.

. . . This is the cup of My Blood, the Blood of the new and ever-lasting covenant. It will be shed for you and all so that sins may be forgiven."

"So that sins may be forgiven." When we celebrate the passion, death and resurrection of the Lord Jesus, we receive the fruit of His intercession, our own redemption and the forgiveness of our sins (see *Col* 1:14). So in each Eucharist we, as a priestly people, intercede:

Lamb of God, You take away the sins of the world: have mercy on us. *(Communion Rite of the Roman Liturgy).*

Intercessory Prayer and Other Prayer Forms

Intercession is related to all prayer forms. In terms of the traditional four characteristics of prayer: praise, petition, thanks and reparation, we like to add an adjective before each of them and so make each of them a description of intercession:

Intercession is the *focused praise,* like the focused rays of a laser beam, where we aim our united praise for a particular need.

It is a *united petition* for others where we unite our hearts, minds and voices for an agreed-upon intention.

It is a *conscious thanks* as we are aware of God's specific action in an event or life of a person and can give thanks with full awareness of His activity.

It is a *resonant reparation* as we feel the burden of another and respond with compassionate intercession.

Supplication is a more intense form of intercession that we see in the life of Jesus, in His priestly prayer (see *Jn* 17:7-26), and on the cross. At times we have expressed this as a lament or as tears or a cry of the heart for needs that are before us singing *"Parce Domine,"* or "Lord have Mercy."

Silence is also a form of intercession. Like Mary, our Mother, we try to listen in love to the Lord and to the needs of our brothers and sisters, and then intercede. Sometimes all we can do is hold our brothers and sisters in our hearts and bring them to the heart of the Lord. At other times it is not a question of either silence or vocalizing our intercession, but rather it is a question of both a loving-listening and an asking the Lord for what is needed. Mary at Cana, because of her listening in love, interceded with her Son to begin His public ministry and to do something about a need. She asked and He changed water into wine. Mary on Calvary stood in silence, holding her Son in her heart.

At the village of Bethany both Martha and Mary interceded. Martha actively pursued Jesus while Mary waited in silence for the Teacher's call; but both asked Jesus, both interceded using the identical words:

> *Lord, if You had been here my brother would never have died* (*Jn* 11:21, 32).

Martha went on to add:

> *Even now, I am sure that God will give You whatever You ask of Him* (*Jn* 11:22).

Silence is a listening in love to both the Lord and to our brothers and sisters and is the preparation for interceding in faith with thanks and praise.

Chapter 5

Interceding Always and Everywhere

Our Lord Jesus and St. Paul exhort us to intercede always and everywhere. Recall the many times that these exhortations are repeated.

- *He told them a parable on the necessity of praying always and not losing heart* (*Lk* 18:1).

- *So I say to you, "Ask and you shall receive; seek and you shall find; knock and it shall be opened to you"* (*Lk* 11:9).

- *Ask and you shall receive that your joy may be full* (*Jn* 16:24).

- *Rejoice always, never cease praying, render constant thanks; such is God's will for you* [note: this "you" is plural] *in Christ Jesus* (*1 Thes* 5:16-18).

- *It is my wish, then, that in every place the men shall offer prayers with blameless hands held aloft, and be free from anger and dissension* (*1 Tim* 2:8).

- *. . . Persevere in prayer* (*Rom* 12:12b).

- *At every opportunity pray in the Spirit, using prayers and petitions of every sort. Pray constantly for all in the holy company* (*Eph* 6:18-19).

- *Present your needs to God in every form of prayer and in petitions full of gratitude* (*Phil* 4:6b).

- *Dedicate yourselves to thankfulness. . . . Whatever you do, whether in speech or in action, do it in the name of the Lord Jesus. Give thanks to God the Father through Him (Col 3:16-17).*

- *Pray perseveringly, be attentive to prayer, and pray in a spirit of thanksgiving (Col 4:2-3).*

Where do we most powerfully respond to this exhortation to intercede always and everywhere? In the celebration, proclamation and offering of the Eucharist! The central prayer of each Eucharist begins with a call to intercede "always and everywhere":

> **Priest: The Lord be with you.**
> People: And also with you.
> **Priest: Lift up your hearts.**
> People: We lift them up to the Lord.
> **Priest: Let us give thanks to the Lord our God.**
> People: It is right to give Him thanks and praise.
> **Priest: Father, all-powerful and ever-living God, we do well *always and everywhere* to give You thanks through Jesus Christ our Lord. . . .**

In the Eucharist, in union with Jesus our eternal High Priest and Victim, we give thanks to the Father—*always and everywhere.*

This became very practical for me when it was pointed out to me how many Masses are offered each day—in fact are going on at each moment around the world. There are over 420,000 priests in the world. Just for the sake of a rough calculation, assume that this means there are 420,000 Masses offered each day—17,500 each hour, 290 each minute, 4 to 5 each second. Four to five Masses begin each second—in the time it takes to say, "Praised be Jesus Christ." A Mass, on an average, takes a half-hour so there are approximately 8 to 9 thousand Masses going on at any moment.

Eight to nine thousand Masses are going on right now! Right now I can unite myself with the Lord Jesus as the Holy Eucharist is being offered to the Father. In addition, I can unite myself with Jesus present in the thousands of tabernacles around the world. The prophetic word given through Malachi is really being fulfilled:

> *For from the rising of the sun, even to its setting, My name is great among the nations; and everywhere they bring sacrifice to My name, a pure offering: for great is My name among all the nations says the Lord of hosts (Malachi 2:11).*

The third Eucharistic Prayer at Mass addresses the Father, paraphrasing this same prophecy:

> From age to age You gather a people to Yourself,
> so that from east to west, a perfect offering may
> be made to the glory of Your name.

This means that at each moment and in every circumstance I can offer the Eucharist. I can offer the Immaculate Victim and in union with Him I can offer myself. As a royal priest I can offer my whole being—body, soul, and spirit. I can offer "always and everywhere" even the least of my sufferings, or rather *especially* my little sufferings, because those are often the only ones I have. In union with the Immaculate Victim, the Eucharistically offered Victim, the eternal Priest and Victim, Jesus Christ, Who offered Himself on Calvary for the salvation of us all—in union with Him my smallest offerings become His and so of the greatest worth and power. These little sufferings are so precious we should not waste them, but rather offer them in union with the one eternal sacrifice going on this very moment in thousands of Masses around the world.

Always and everywhere I can offer up the present situation. Nothing is too small to offer, nothing insignificant when offered Eucharistically, when offered in union with Jesus for the salvation of souls to the glory of the Father. It is called intercession. We are all called to it.

Chapter 6

The General Intercessions
of the Eucharist

The Liturgy of the Eucharist is the great act of intercession of
the Church. By interceding, the Church exercises her role as
Bride of Christ, reigning and ruling with Him. Like the queen she
is, the Church intercedes with her all-powerful King. These intercessions come in various forms.

In addition to the *sacrificial action* of the Eucharist, the
Eucharistic *prayers* (Canon of the Mass) are themselves intercessory. Moreover the three orations of the Mass: the opening
prayer, the prayer over the gifts, and the prayer after communion
express the particular needs of the feast or season.

Then, in addition to the sacrificial actions and prayers of the
Eucharist, the Church intercedes in the *general intercessions.*

> In the general intercessions or prayer of the faithful,
> the people exercise their priestly function by interced-
> ing for all mankind. It is appropriate that this prayer
> be included in all Masses celebrated with a congrega-
> tion, so that intercessions may be made for the
> Church, for civil authorities, for those oppressed by
> various needs, for all mankind, and for the salvation of
> the world. . . . The priest directs the prayers: with a
> brief introduction he invites the people to pray, and
> after the intentions he says the concluding prayer. . . .
> The congregation makes its petition either by a com-
> mon response after each intention or by silent prayers
> (*General Instruction of the Roman Missal,* 45-47. See
> Appendix III).

The *Liturgy of the Hours* extends these general intercessions in
the celebration of Morning and Evening Prayer. The intercessions

from the Evening Prayer of Ascension Thursday to Pentecost make a marvelous novena of prayers in preparation for the feast of Pentecost (see Appendix III). This week of preparation is the one official and original novena which the Church celebrates.

In the Liturgy, the Church responds to the command of the Lord to pray for all our needs (see *Lk* 11:1-13) and to pray always and not lose heart (see *Lk* 18:1). St. Paul exhorted the Church to pray constantly for all, as we noted previously, and all of these intercessions are interwoven into the Eucharist.

> *First of all I urge that petitions, prayers and interces-*
> *sions and thanksgiving be offered for all men, espe-*
> *cially for kings and those in authority that we may be*
> *able to lead undisturbed and tranquil lives in perfect*
> *piety and dignity. Prayer of this kind is good, and God*
> *our savior is pleased with it, for He wants all men to*
> *be saved and come to know the truth (1 Tim 2:1-4).*

How beautifully and powerfully the Divine Liturgy (Byzantine Rite) (see Appendix III) repeatedly sends up its intercessory prayers to the throne of the Father, for all mankind, for all kinds of needs.

The solemn intercessions of the Good Friday celebration of the Lord's Passion (Roman Rite) (see Appendix III) illustrate the Church's way of interceding for all mankind. The priest presents the intention, all respond with prayer in silence, then the priest collects our prayer in the oration. This pattern of intercession is repeated for the ten intentions presented: for the Church, for the Pope, for the clergy and laity of the Church, for those preparing for baptism, for the unity of Christians, for the Jewish people, for those who do not believe in Christ, for those who do not believe in God, for all in public office, for those in special need (the sick, the dying, travelers, those deprived of liberty. . . .)

The pattern of the Church's intercessory prayer is a pattern that we can all extend and follow throughout the day: we can express our intention to the Lord succinctly, pray in our hearts and then express it further in a formal prayer.

The author of the *Letter to the Hebrews* exhorts us:

> *Through Him [Jesus] let us continually offer God a*
> *sacrifice of praise, that is, the fruit of lips which*
> *acknowledge His name (Heb 13:15).*

Chapter 7

Interceding in the Presence of the Eucharistic Lord

A mystic once related: "As Jesus is truly in Heaven, so also is He truly present on earth in the Eucharist with His Body, His Blood, His Soul and His Divinity."

So coming into the presence of the Eucharist to intercede is to come into the presence of the Lord Himself. We enter into the radiance of His presence that penetrates us and transforms our intercession. Coming into the presence of the Lord in the Eucharist is like being irradiated with the rays of the sun. So in a sense, our intercession before the Blessed Sacrament is above all a presence—our presence to His presence, like a plant in the sun drawing energy to grow and bear fruit.

The more we expose ourselves to His radiating presence, the more we are transformed into His image. Through us then, Jesus makes Himself present again, immolates Himself anew and gives Himself to souls. In this way we become truly intercessors before the Father. Would that we be fully transformed and radiate His presence!

Various mystics have related that a time is coming when the Church and world will be renewed and we will be a Eucharistic people. I think this means that Jesus in the Eucharist will be the focal point of our lives—that our gatherings, our worship, and intercessions will center on His Eucharistic presence among us.

Intercession in the presence of the Blessed Sacrament is really an extension of the Mass itself in that we continue the offering, the proclamation, and the celebration as we intercede with adoration and thanksgiving. We can extend the moments of the Mass, that are so precious and which pass all too quickly, by dwelling on them in the presence of the Eucharistic Lord in a contemplative and worshipful way. I think that it is also important to consider liturgies such as Benediction of the Blessed Sacrament and Eucharistic processions as extensions of the Mass, which is the heartbeat and central liturgy of the Church.

A renewed devotion to the Eucharistic presence is beginning to flourish in many parishes and it is taking the form of perpetual adoration of the Blessed Sacrament. Parishioners are responding to the challenge to sign up for an hour of adoration each week, covering the 168 hours of the week. The people's generous response and the graces flowing from this perpetual adoration have been encouraging signs that a renewal is taking place through Eucharistic adoration and intercession.

There are several resources available for starting Eucharistic adoration:

Perpetual Adoration Committee, St. Thomas More Church, 10330 Hillcroft, Houston, TX 77096.

Fr. Martin Lucia is the director for the *Apostolate for Perpetual Adoration.* This outstanding ministry provides workshops and materials for initiating programs in parishes. They can be contacted at P.O. Box 46502, Mount Clemens, MI 48046.

A number of publishers provide meditation and prayer booklets designed specifically for use at visits to the Blessed Sacrament. One such booklet, titled *An Hour with Jesus,* is available from The Riehle Foundation, P.O. Box 7, Milford, OH 45150. A $2.00 donation is suggested.

Chapter 8

How to Make a Holy Hour

So, you could not stay awake with me for even an hour? Be on guard, and pray that you may not undergo the test (*Mt* 26:40-41).

There are different ways to "watch one hour" with the Lord. Here we will consider spending an hour in the presence of the Blessed Sacrament. We call it a Holy Hour because it is in the presence of the Holy Eucharist. There are also different ways to make a Holy Hour: before the tabernacle alone or with others, or in the presence of the exposed Blessed Sacrament privately or as a community led by a priest or deacon. In these considerations let us consider first the Church's teaching on the adoration of the Blessed Sacrament and then consider various possibilities of what can be done in spending the hour with the Lord.

The Church's Teaching on the Adoration of the Holy Eucharist

The Church's teaching on the worship of the Holy Eucharist is found in *The Rites of the Catholic Church,* as revised by the Decree of the Second Vatican Ecumenical Council and published by the authority of Pope Paul VI. The following is a gleaning of teachings from Chapter III.

Both private and public devotion toward the Eucharist are strongly encouraged. Devotions should take their origin from the liturgy of the Eucharistic sacrifice and lead people back to the liturgy. The presence of Christ is derived from the sacrifice and is directed toward sacramental spiritual communion. Prayer before the Lord sacramentally present extends the union with

Christ which the faithful have received in communion. It renews the covenant which in turn moves them to maintain in their lives what they have received by faith and by sacraments. Everyone should be concerned with good deeds and with pleasing God so that he or she may imbue the world with the Christian spirit and be a witness of Christ in the midst of human society.

Public Adoration

The Church also teaches about what is to be done during the time of public adoration conducted by a priest or deacon. Here, again, is a gleaning of what is asked.

During the exposition there should be prayers, songs and readings to direct the faithful to the worship of the Lord, to encourage a prayerful spirit. There should be readings from scripture with a homily or brief exhortation to develop a better understanding of the Eucharistic mystery. It is also desirable for people to respond to the word of God by singing and to spend periods of time in religious silence. Part of the liturgy of the hours may be celebrated to extend the praise and thanksgiving of Holy Mass.

The elements of prayer, the scriptures, praise and silence are all an integral part of public adoration. All the elements of the public adoration should acknowledge the marvelous presence of Christ in the sacrament and foster the worship which is due to Christ in spirit and truth. Such public adoration of the Blessed Sacrament must clearly express its relationship to the Mass.

Private Adoration

Certainly the teachings of the Church in regard to public adoration can be made use of in private adoration to aid our spiritual communion with the presence of the Lord.

But now, I want to turn to my personal reflections. The key word that stands out for me is *presence*. To "watch one hour" with the Lord we need to be present to the One Who is present to us. Certainly bodily presence is a first step, and at times that is all we are capable of, but we are called to more. To please the Lord we need to be present with our hearts. This means a loving awareness of Who is present. It means a silent presence—not analyzing, thinking, nor just saying prayers with our lips. It means being in the Heart of Mary Our Mother, trusting and rejoicing.

If only I could spend a whole hour watching in silent presence with my heart present to Him, I would rejoice and give thanks. But even a few short moments of such presence to the presence of the Lord is a precious treasure. To seek the Lord with our whole heart is what prayer is all about.

It is in this silence that the Lord speaks to us. To be silently present to the One Who is present is what it means to listen and watch one hour with Him. If all we did was be silent for an hour it would be a marvelous time of prayer. It is in silent presence that we can be irradiated by the radiation of His Eucharistic presence. We all need radiation therapy, and to receive it we only need to be present. Just as in sun bathing we only need to be present to the ultraviolet radiation of the sun.

We all need the time of silence, especially in our age that is so heavily bombarded with words, words, words—from reading materials, radio, audio cassettes and TV. We all need a time of silence to listen to the Lord Who speaks in a very special language called silence.

How beautifully Blessed Faustina describes her long talks with the Lord without saying a word (*Diary,* #411). Truly silence is the language of God:

> Silence is so powerful a language that it reaches the throne of the living God. Silence is His language, though secret, yet living and powerful (*Diary,* #888).

> In silence I tell You everything, Lord, because the language of love is without words . . . (*Diary,* #1489).

We all need to spend silent time in the presence of the Eucharistic Lord to let Him love us—to let Him minister to us with His healing, merciful love. Yes, we also need the time of silent presence to love Him and to make reparation for our sins and those of the whole world. It is a powerful and effective way to thank Him for His gift of mercy to us and at the same time to be "merciful to Him" since the Lord continues to suffer in His Body, the Church.

Eucharistic Prayers

There are classical prayers in preparation for Holy Mass and in Thanksgiving after Mass given in Appendix I of *The Sacramentary of the Roman Missal* that can help inspire our presence before the Blessed Sacrament. There are also prayers from the Diary of Blessed Faustina that are especially suitable during Eucharistic adoration and can be found in *The Divine Mercy Message and Devotion* booklet:

• The Chaplet of The Divine Mercy
• Praises of The Divine Mercy
• At the Feet of Christ in the Eucharist
• For the Conversion of Sinners
• For Divine Mercy

The Chaplet of The Divine Mercy holds a special place of honor as a Eucharistic prayer because it is a continuation of the offering of the Mass. And in turn the simple prayer "Jesus, Mercy!" is a continuation of the Chaplet, a plea for God's mercy for every moment of need.

How to Begin a Private Holy Hour

Start with the body-language of a gesture of profound adoration. Invoke the Holy Spirit to fill you with His gift of praise. Unite your heart with the Heart of Mary so that you praise the Lord with the Heart of His mother. Call upon the angels and saints to help you to unite with their heavenly praise and worship. Let your heart be aglow with the Lord's radiant presence and then follow the longing of your heart. Love Him, thank Him and praise Him, Who is present and loves you.

Be still and know that I am God (Ps 46:10, RSV).

What About Distractions?

The distractions will usually be there. To combat them, we can use a litany of mercy in our daily prayer time, especially if we are distracted and anxious about situations in our lives.

How do we do this? Let me suggest a method that has helped me. Simply begin by asking the Holy Spirit to pray in you, and then respond to each of the distractions and anxieties—from whatever source—with short prayers such as: "Jesus, mercy" or "Jesus, I trust in You."

Imagine that each of the distractions, anxieties, fears, or hurts is a slide in a slide-show. Project one "slide" at a time on the wall and pray your response, and then move on to the next "slide." You will be surprised when suddenly you have run through all your slides and are at peace in the presence of the Lord in your heart.

How do you End a Holy Hour?

A good way to end a holy hour is to *thank* the Lord for His presence and make any notes on graces or resolutions received during the hour. Then, again, express your adoration with your whole body and soul.

The material in this chapter is available as a leaflet (code HH) from:
The Marian Helpers Center, Stockbridge, MA 01263, phone: 1-(800) 462-7426.

Chapter 9

To Intercede is to be as Eucharist

Over the years of interceding for the needs of brother priests, I have been coming to the fuller awareness that intercession is Eucharistic, in fact, to intercede is to *be as Eucharist.* I will try to further explain.

The lives and writings of two mystics from Mexico and one from Poland have challenged me in this regard: Conchita (Maria Concepcion Cabrera de Armida), Mother Auxilia de la Cruz, O.S.S.E., and Blessed Faustina Kowalska.

Conchita

The book *Conchita: a Mother's Spiritual Diary* edited by Rev. M. M. Philipon, O.P. (Alba House, 2187 Victory Blvd., Staten Is., NY 10314) has been a very special grace for me. It not only confirmed what was happening within me but has opened up new vistas. Conchita (1862-1937) was a mother of nine children, a mystic and a writer. For fifty years she wrote what the Lord dictated to her, recording this in over a hundred volumes: teachings on virtues and vices, the cross and the Eucharist, priesthood, the Holy Spirit, Mary and the Church, and the Holy Trinity. She founded several religious communities and "works of the cross." Father Marie-Michel Philipon, O.P. spent the last years of his life studying her life and writings. He points out that "By the profundity of the sublimeness of her writings, Conchita rivals St. Catherine of Sienna or Teresa of Avila. One of the Commission charged with examining her [writings] in 1913 in Rome declared: 'She is extraordinary of the extraordinary'!" Father Philipon shows throughout his book how her writings anticipated teachings of the Second Vatican Council.

May the following samples of Conchita's Diary serve to give a taste of the richness of the teachings given her:

The most sublime aspect in Christ is His Priesthood centered on the Cross. The Eucharist and the Cross constitute one and the same mystery. The first form of union consists in living the life of Christ by grace and the second by imitation. For me, I repeat, the aspect I must imitate, in virtue of the mystical incarnation, is His Priesthood centered on the Cross. The monasteries of the Cross (Oasis) are but one vast Mass (*Diary,* Dec. 28, 1923).

"Briefly," says Father Philipon, "the mystical incarnation (Conchita's central grace) is a grace of identification with Christ, Priest and Victim, a grace which makes Him continue on in the members of His Mystical Body His mission of glorifier of the Father and Savior of men. It is a special grace of transformation into the priestly soul of Christ. The principal act of the mystical incarnation is the offering, not in two acts but in one, the oblation of Christ to His Father and the total oblation of our own life for the salvation of the world and for the greatest glory of the Trinity."

The Lord reportedly explained to Conchita the mystery of the cross and the Eucharist and Mary:

It was at the Cross that Mary saw My Church born, that she accepted in her heart, in the person of St. John, all the priests in place of Me, and further, to be the mother of all mankind (*Diary,* April 8, 1928).

But I have need of an army of holy priests transformed into Myself, who exhale virtues and attract souls with the good aroma of Jesus Christ. I have need of other Christs on earth, forming one sole Christ in My Church. . . . (*Diary,* Dec 29, 1927).

The fire must be rekindled and this will be done only by the Holy Spirit, by the divine medium of the Word, offering Him to the Father and asking for mercy (*Diary,* Sept. 23, 1927).

Conchita kept on writing again and again: "The Church and world has need of a 'new Pentecost,' a second Pentecost, a priestly Pentecost, an interior Pentecost." This was fifty years before the Second Vatican Council.

Father Philipon concluded his book saying, "Conchita's prophetic mission is that of recalling to the modern and materialistic world, avid for liberty, that it will be saved only by a NEW PENTECOST and by the GOSPEL OF THE CROSS." (p. 251).

Mother Auxilia

The works and life of Mother Maria Auxilia de la Cruz, O.S.S.E., of Mexico continue the same teachings. Mother Auxilia (1891-1974) was a close friend of Conchita and had the same spiritual director, Archbishop Martinez, primate of Mexico. In her book *Living The Eucharist* (*Vida Eucharistica,* 1931, Oblates of the Blessed Sacrament, Eden Hill, Stockbridge, MA 01262) Mother Auxilia shows how a person is called to be as Eucharistic—to be a living "host" (*alma Hostia*)—a Eucharistically offered soul in union with and transformed by and into Jesus the Eucharistically offered Victim. She showed how a soul develops in the spiritual life following the steps of the Eucharistic action: set apart as pure, offered and transformed, to be given in communion for the salvation of souls and the glory of the Father.

The transformation of the bread into the Body of the Lord is by the fire of the Holy Spirit. It is the fire which consumed Christ's self-offering on the cross. It is the fire of divine love, the fire of the Holy Spirit that transforms us into "living hosts."

The Oblates of the Blessed Sacrament founded by Mother Auxilia try to live this life of being Eucharistically offered victims especially for the sake of the shepherds of the Church. Mother Guadalupe, one of the first novices, told me that Mother Auxilia's last words to her, ten days before her death in 1974, were, "Call on the Holy Spirit always. Call Him—Come! Come! You can do nothing without Him."

I am becoming more and more aware that a person who wants to become an intercessor, who wants to fully exercise the royal priesthood, needs to become Eucharistic—set aside, blessed, broken and given for others. As intercessors, we need to allow ourselves to be transformed by the power of the Holy Spirit so that united with Jesus our Head and eternal High Priest we can offer ourselves, in a sense saying, "Take and eat. This is my body given for you. Take and drink. This is my blood poured out for you, for the forgiveness of sins, for the salvation of all."

In this way, through the power of the Holy Spirit, like Mary, we offer ourselves, our whole being as created by God (this is the Hebrew meaning of "body"). In this way we will respond to the solemn exhortation of St. Paul:

> *I beg you through the mercies of God to offer your bodies as a living sacrifice holy and acceptable to God your spiritual worship (Rom 12:1).*

In this way we will come to experience the reality of:

> *All of us, gazing on the Lord's glory with unveiled faces, are being transformed from glory to glory, into His very image by the Lord Who is the Spirit (2 Cor 3:18).*

In this way each of us comes to know that: "*I have been cruci-fied with Christ and the life I live now is not my own. Christ is living in me*" (*Gal* 2:19b-20).

As the Eucharist retains the external appearances of the bread and wine, hiding both the divinity and humanity of Jesus, we too, in this Eucharistic transformation, retain all our exterior appear-ances and weaknesses, which hide the power and the presence of the Lord. "*It is no longer I who live, but Christ lives in me*" (*Gal* 2:20).

> *This treasure we posses in earthen vessels, to make it clear that its surpassing power comes from God and not from us (2 Cor 4:7).*
>
> *. . . for in weakness power reaches perfection (2 Cor 12:9b).*

Blessed Faustina Kowalska

Blessed Maria Faustina of the Most Blessed Sacrament (her full name) has been called "the great apostle of Divine Mercy in our time" by Pope John Paul II. Ample evidence of this is given both by her diary, which records the message and devotion of

Divine Mercy and by the effect it has been having on people who read it, making them apostles of Divine Mercy.

A very special aspect of Sister's life was her desire to be transformed into a *living Host,* a wafer, hidden and broken to be given to others:

> Jesus, transform me, miserable and sinful as I am, into Your own self (for You can do all things), and give me to Your Eternal Father. I want to be a *sacrificial host* before You, but an ordinary wafer to people. I want the fragrance of my sacrifice to be known to You alone (*Diary,* #483).

> Transform me in Yourself, O Jesus, that I may be a living sacrifice and pleasing to You. *I desire to atone at each moment for poor sinners* (*Diary,* #908).

Jesus answered her prayers telling her: "You are a living host, pleasing to the Heavenly Father" (*Diary,* #1826). Sister Faustina felt this transformation as a holy fire present in her ways:

> All the good that is in me is due to Holy Communion. I owe everything to it. I feel this holy fire has transformed me completely. Oh, how happy I am to be a dwelling for You, O Lord! My heart is a temple in which You dwell continually (*Diary,* #1392).

The experience of being a *living host,* hidden, broken, and given was the central experience of her life. But, this experience was based on the *union* of love with the living God. And this union was most profoundly experienced in conjunction with the Holy Eucharist, either during Mass and Holy Communion, or during adoration of the Blessed Sacrament. Her union with the Lord was, in His words, as a bride:

> Here, I am entirely yours, soul, body and divinity as your Bridegroom. You know what love demands, one thing only, reciprocity (*Diary,* #1770).

Chapter 10

The Echo of the Lord's Prayer and Communion Rite of Mass in The Divine Mercy Message and Devotion

The Communion Rite of the Roman Mass begins with the Lord's Prayer. It is echoed, reflected upon and expanded in the prayers that follow and culminates in the reception of Holy Communion. It is also echoed, continued, extended and made present to each moment of the day through the Divine Mercy message and devotion as given to Blessed Faustina.

It is inspiring to reflect on and pray over the parallels between the Communion Rite and the Divine Mercy message and devotion. Let us walk through the Communion Rite and then through some of the parallels.

Communion Rite

The *Our Father* is the Lord's own prayer. When His disciples asked Jesus to teach them to pray (see *Lk* 11:1), He shared His own prayer with them. For this reason it is the most important prayer of the Church. The Church officially prays the Our Father three times a day: at Holy Mass, and at Morning and Evening Prayer in the Liturgy of the Hours.

> In the *Eucharistic liturgy* the Lord's Prayer appears as the prayer of the whole Church and there reveals its full meaning and efficacy. Placed between the *anaphora* (the Eucharistic prayer) and the communion, the Lord's Prayer sums up on the one hand all the petitions and intercessions expressed . . . and, on

the other, knocks at the door of the Banquet of the kingdom which sacramental communion anticipates (*Catechism of the Catholic Church,* #2770.) [1]

As a priestly, Eucharistic people the Lord's prayer is our most important intercessory prayer because in it we ask that the Father's will be done and His kingdom come among us.

The essence of the Lord's Prayer, which begins the Communion Rite, can be illustrated with a flow diagram describing the words "Father, Your kingdom come":

```
                          YOUR
FATHER ──────────────►    KINGDOM
                          COME
```

The prayer addresses the Father as *Our* Father, *Abba* (dearest Father), the Father of us all. The great petition of the prayer is that His kingdom come, which is the reign of Jesus His beloved Son among us. The establishing of His kingdom in our hearts and in the world is *how* the Father is hallowed on earth as in heaven. This is *how* His will is done:

```
              HALLOWED
OUR           BE YOUR NAME ────────►    YOUR
FATHER ───                             KINGDOM
              YOUR WILL BE DONE         COME!
              ON EARTH AS
              IT IS IN HEAVEN
```

The petition to establish His kingdom *on earth as it is in heaven* is a Eucharistic petition. We are asking that the heavenly, eternal, and perpetual presence of the sacrificed Lamb of God be made present among us here on earth as it is in heaven. In other words, we are asking to become a living Eucharist, a *presence* of the mystical Body of Christ here on earth. In this petition for the kingdom we are asking that the Lord reign and be present among us *now* so that His will be done and He may be glorified.

---

[1] I recommend and strongly urge you, the reader, to study the final section of the *Catechism of the Catholic Church,* on *Christian Prayer.* It is the best and most authoritative presentation on prayer I have ever read. It is based on Sacred Scripture, tradition, the Magisterium of the Church, and the writings of saints; and it is written in a way that inspires the heart and illumines the mind. It culminates in the final section in a full and beautiful teaching on the Lord's Prayer.

The "kingdom," the reign of Jesus, is the form of the Lord's Prayer used in the Eucharist celebration. A variant used for the baptismal rite asks "may Your Holy Spirit come down upon us and cleanse us" (*Jerusalem Bible*, footnote on *Lk* 11:2).

The next set of petitions of the Lord's Prayer is directed against the kingdom of the Evil One. We pray not to be put to the test and ask for deliverance from the Evil One; in effect we ask for the destruction of the kingdom of the Evil One:

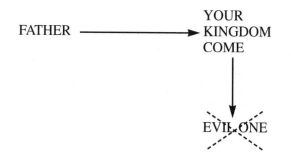

The two conditions for destroying the Evil One's kingdom are to trust and be merciful. We trust by relying on the Lord's daily bread today, and we are merciful by forgiving one another:

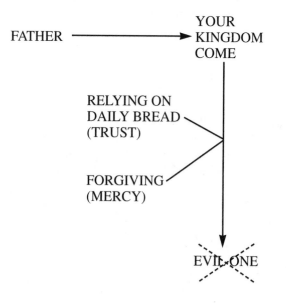

The prayer that follows (embolism) expands, echoes, and continues the Lord's Prayer:

> Deliver us, Lord, from every evil, and grant us peace in our day. In Your mercy keep us free from sin and protect us from all anxiety as we wait with joyful hope for the coming of our Savior, Jesus Christ.

The Church asks for deliverance and protection from the obstacles to God's kingdom among us and asks for the fullness of all blessings, that is, peace and mercy in expectation of the glorious reign of Jesus. This is all a gift of Divine Mercy.

All then respond with the great doxology:

> For the kingdom, the power and the glory are Yours, now and forever. Amen.

The priest prays for peace, asking the Lord look not at our sins but rather on the faith of the Church. The peace the Church prays for is the peace that Jesus gives us (see *Jn* 14:27). It is the peace with which the resurrected Jesus greets His disciples on Easter Sunday night: *"Peace be with you"* (*Jn* 20:19,21). It is this peace which He bestows on them by breathing on them the Holy Spirit, giving them the power to forgive sins. This peace is the fullness of all blessing, the Holy Spirit, the Spirit of Mercy. This is the victory gift of Jesus—the Spirit of Peace, of Mercy, and of Unity—the gift of His Holy Spirit.

This is the *Peace* we extend to one another at that point in the Mass.

Then we all cry out to the Lamb of God, Jesus, Who is both Priest and Victim to have mercy on us sinners and grant us peace. Meanwhile the priest breaks the consecrated bread and mingles a fragment with the precious Blood, praying for eternal life to those who receive It. He continues with his personal preparation for Holy Communion asking to be freed from sin and evil, and to be kept faithful to Christ's teaching and never be separated from Him.

The priest then raises the host saying:

This is the Lamb of God Who takes away the sins of the world. Happy are those who are called to His supper.

All add:

Lord, I am not worthy to receive You, but only say the word and I shall be healed.

After receiving the precious Body and Blood of the Lord with reverence, we are left to contemplate these profound gifts and mysteries.

Parallels of the Divine Mercy Message

The message of Divine Mercy, that is, to trust the Lord and be merciful, is an echo and a continuation of the Communion Rite beginning with the Lord's Prayer.

The Lord's prayer can also be expressed in terms of trust and mercy:

Our Father, *"rich in mercy"* (*Eph* 2:4) may Your will to *"have mercy on all"* (*Rom* 11:32) be done in us so that Your name may be hallowed on earth as in heaven. May Your kingdom of Mercy Incarnate be present among us. As we trust in You each day and mercifully forgive one another, deliver us from the kingdom of the Evil One.

The Lord's Prayer as a prayer of trust and mercy can also be expressed in a shorter form:

Father of all mercies (see *2 Cor* 1:3), may Your mercy be made present by our trust in You and our mercy toward one another.

The Church asks for the fullness of the blessing of all mercy, that is, *Peace*, the gift of the Holy Spirit Himself—a peace and mercy that will keep us free from sin and protect us from all anxiety as we wait for the glorious *coming* of Jesus Christ. The Divine Mercy message is given to us, in order to prepare for this coming. (*Diary*, #635, 848, 1146, 1588).

As noted above, in preparation for the Eucharist, the priest prays the words of Jesus at the Last Supper (see *Jn* 14:27) and Easter Sunday night (see *Jn* 20:19-20) and extends that peace to all. Blessed Faustina records the words of Our Lord about peace:

> Mankind will have no peace until it turns with trust to My mercy (*Diary,* #300).

And again:

> Tell aching mankind to snuggle close to My Merciful Heart, and I will fill it with peace (*Diary,* #1074).

When we call upon the "Lamb of God," we call upon Jesus Who is both our High Priest and Victim and Who is the source of all mercy. From the pierced side of the risen Lamb of God comes the flow of blood and water, the sacramental life of the Church.

This is the Lamb of God lifted up before our eyes by the celebrant. We should all cry out our unworthiness to receive Him in Holy Communion. All of us are unworthy, but God in His great mercy has humbled Himself to be the Lamb that we receive and consume, and so are transformed. We should not just receive Him, but we should enter into communion with Him—a "common union-in-Christ." According to St. Augustine (*Confessions*), we are to become what we eat! We are to become, more and more, the very image of God, living icons of trust and mercy.

The Parallels of the Divine Mercy Devotions

True devotions lead us to a transformation, an inner conversion to become images of what we are devoted to. By our devotion to the Divine Mercy, we are to become "living icons of Mercy"—a living presence of trust and mercy.

Like Blessed Faustina we are to be *living images* of the merciful Savior. She prayed:

> I want to be completely transformed into Your mercy and to be Your living reflection. O Lord, may the greatest of all divine attributes, that of Your unfathomable mercy, pass through my heart and soul to my neighbor (*Diary,* #163).

Like Blessed Faustina, each of us is to become as *Living Eucharist,* a "wafer" blessed, broken and given for others. In this way we truly extend the Mass to each moment.

Like Blessed Faustina, we are to become a *living chaplet of Divine Mercy* by offering all our sufferings in union with the passion of Jesus in atonement for our sins and those of the whole world. Our offering alone is a mere nothing, but united with Christ, it is a powerful plea for mercy on us and on the whole world. Reading Sister Faustina's life story can be a truly uplifting spiritual encounter. She was the epitome of intercession.

Our Lord told Blessed Faustina that we are to radiate His mercy to others:

> Tell (all people), My daughter, that I am Love and Mercy itself. When a soul approaches Me with trust, I will fill it with such an abundance of graces, that it cannot contain them within itself, but radiates them to others (*Diary,* #1074).

In other words, we are to radiate His mercy! His peace! His forgiveness! We are to become what the Church expresses in the prayer after the Lord's Prayer:

> Delivered from evil and filled with peace and mercy, freed from sin and anxiety, we joyfully wait for the glorious coming of Jesus Christ our Lord.

This is the peace and mercy Jesus gives us on Easter Sunday night as recorded in the Gospel of St. John (see *Jn* 20) and proclaimed on the Feast of Divine Mercy. This is the peace the priest blesses us with and then we exchange with one another at the kiss of peace. This is the peace and mercy we receive and enter into communion with. This is the peace and mercy we are to radiate and share with others.

Our part is to turn to Jesus with trust, receive His mercy with thanksgiving and share His mercy with joy.

Yes, both the Divine Mercy message of trust and mercy and the devotions to the Divine Mercy echo, extend, and continue the offering of the Immaculate Victim of the altar and the whole of the Communion Rite of the Mass. We are to imitate what we celebrate and become what we consume. We are to be living icons of Mercy, here on earth, hallowing the name of the Eternal Father, fulfilling His will and striving to have mercy on all. Thus we make mercy present, and make His kingdom among us present by our trust in Jesus and by our lives of mercy toward one another. In this way we defeat the kingdom of the Evil One and give all glory to God:

> For the kingdom, the power and the glory are Yours,
> now and forever. Amen.

Chapter 11

The Intercession of Suffering

The intercession of suffering needs to be considered as clearly as possible. It is a difficult topic to consider because it is associated with the pain of actual suffering and the imagined pain of future suffering which complicates the issue. This type of intercession is known under various names, such as victim intercession, redemptive suffering, vicarious suffering, and victim souls. This type of suffering in intercession for others has a firm basis in scripture and in the long tradition of the saints, but is not something that is frequently discussed or frequently sought after!

This whole question of suffering has been of interest to me over the years and I reflected on the meaning of suffering in a book titled, *The Good News of Suffering: Mercy and Salvation for All* (Liturgical Press, Collegeville, MN, 1981). The Holy Father, Pope John Paul II, has also written on the subject: *The Christian Meaning of Human Suffering* (*Salvifici Doloris*, Feb. 11, 1984, an Apostolic Letter, is available from Origins or from the Daughters of St. Paul). This very special letter from the pope ties together the role of suffering and of intercession for the salvation of the world. It explains the Sacred Scriptures that deal with suffering in light of our own human experience of suffering. It is a masterpiece and calls for our study.

One of the scriptures that Pope John Paul II develops is taken from St. Paul's Letter to the Colossians:

> *Even now I find my joy in the suffering I endure for you. In my own flesh I fill up what is lacking in the sufferings of Christ for the sake of His body, the church* (*Col* 1:24).

Another text that he develops is

46

Yes, God so loved the world that He gave His only Son, that whoever believes in Him may not die but may have eternal life (Jn 3:16).

It is love that transformed this total and sacrificial giving of His Son.

The Holy Father directly addresses the question of suffering for others and actually speaks of it as a *vocation and a call.*

> For Christ does not answer directly and He does not answer in the abstract this human questioning about the meaning of suffering. Man hears Christ's saving answer as he himself gradually becomes a sharer in the sufferings of Christ.

> The answer which comes through this sharing, by way of the interior encounter with the Master, is in itself *something more than the mere abstract answer* to the question about the meaning of suffering. For it is above all a call. It is a vocation. Christ does not explain in the abstract the reasons for suffering, but before all else He says: "Follow me!" Come! Take part through your suffering in this work of saving the world, a salvation achieved through My suffering! Through My cross! Gradually, *as the individual takes up his cross,* spiritually uniting himself to the cross of Christ, the salvific meaning of suffering is revealed before him. He does not discover this meaning at his own human level, but at the level of the suffering of Christ. At the same time, however, from this level of Christ the salvific meaning of suffering *descends to man's level* and becomes, in a sense, the individual's personal response. It is then that man finds in his suffering interior peace and even spiritual joy.

> St. Paul speaks of such joy in the letter to the Colossians: "I rejoice in my sufferings for your sake." A source of joy is found in the *overcoming of the sense of the uselessness of suffering,* a feeling that is sometimes very strongly rooted in human suffering.

This feeling not only consumes the person interiorly, but seems to make him a burden to others. The person feels condemned to receive help and assistance from others, and at the same time seems useless to himself. The discovery of the salvific meaning of suffering in union with Christ *transforms* this depressing *feeling*. Faith in sharing in the suffering of Christ brings with it the interior certainty that the suffering person "completes what is lacking in Christ's afflictions"; the certainty that in the spiritual dimension of the work of Redemption *he is serving,* like Christ, *the salvation of his brothers and sisters.* Therefore, he is carrying out an irreplaceable service. In the Body of Christ, which is ceaselessly born of the cross of the Redeemer, it is precisely suffering permeated by the spirit of Christ's sacrifice that is *the irreplaceable mediator and author of the good things* which are indispensable for the world's salvation. It is suffering, more than anything else, which clears the way for the grace which transforms human souls. Suffering, more than anything else, makes present in the history of humanity the powers of the Redemption. In that "cosmic" struggle between the spiritual powers of good and evil, spoken of in the letter to the Ephesians, human sufferings, united to the redemptive suffering of Christ, *constitute a special support for the powers of good,* and open the way to the victory of these salvific powers.

And so the Church sees in all Christ's suffering brothers and sisters as it were a *multiple subject of His supernatural power.* How often is it precisely to them that the pastors of the Church appeal, and precisely from them that they seek help and support! The Gospel of suffering is being written unceasingly, and it speaks unceasingly with the words of this strange paradox: the springs of divine power gush forth precisely in the midst of human weakness. Those who share in the sufferings of Christ preserve in their own sufferings a very special *particle of the infinite treasure* of the world's Redemption, and can share this treasure with others. The more a person is threatened by sin, the heavier the structures of sin which today's world brings with it—the greater is the eloquence which human suffering possesses in itself. And the more the Church feels the need to have recourse to the value of human sufferings for the salvation of the world. (John Paul II, Feb. 11, 1984, *Salvifici Doloris* 26, 27)

In a homily addressed to some 400 sick people gathered in the Basilica of St. Peter in Rome, John Paul II asked that they offer their sufferings for the conversion of the world and then referred to his Apostolic Letter published that same day (*L'Osservatore Romano*, English Edition, February 27, 1984). He stated:

Dear sick! Offer your sufferings to the Lord with love and with generosity for *the conversion of the world!* Man must understand the gravity of sin, of offending God, and be converted to Him Who, through love, created him and calls him to everlasting happiness.

Accept your pains with courage and confidence, also for all those who are suffering in the world because of religious persecutions, because of painful political and social situations; or who are victims of the corruption of customs and the reigning climate of materialism and hedonism; or who wander without faith and without certainty in indifference or religious denial. You too, like Jesus on the Cross, can obtain graces of light, repentance, conversion and salvation for these brothers and sisters.

Finally, I exhort you to an ever more *intense and deep love for the Church,* which always, but especially today, must be wholly united in truth, in charity and in discipline.

You who are sick, who see how confused and threatened humanity is in its search for certainty and truth, also share in a special way in this mysterious passion; therefore pray and suffer for the Church, for bishops, for priests, for vocations, for seminarians and for

> those responsible for priestly and religious formation.
> The Church needs people who pray and love in silence
> and in suffering: and in your infirmity, you can truly
> be these apostles!

Sufferings for others is a special calling and gift. It is a gift that
is to be received preferably by spiritually mature souls who are
under a spiritual director. We ought to support our brothers and
sisters who have been called to this vocation with our love and
prayer, because "Suffering, in fact, is always a trial—at times a
very hard one" (John Paul II, *Salvifici Doloris,* 23). We ought not
to assume too quickly that we are victims because we are suffering; rather we should more quickly examine ourselves and repent
of our sins and ask God's forgiveness. At other times we should
seek healing to remove the obstacles that prevent us from know-
ing and experiencing God's love for us. When we have received
sufficient healing to know God's love for us, then we can begin
to discern God's call to unite more fully with Him in the ministry
of the cross.

Over the years of interceding for the Church and especially
priests, many brothers and sisters have shared with me the vocation they have responded to as they offer their sufferings in union
with Christ crucified for the salvation of others. I have been edi-
fied by their faith and generosity and am deeply grateful for the
support they have been to me and many other priests.

Of course, all of us can offer our sufferings with Christ, no
matter how small they are, no matter what type they are, whether
they are physical, emotional, or spiritual. Suffering offered in
union with Christ is very precious to the Lord. Don't waste it.
Offer it up with Christ for the salvation of souls.

Chapter 12

Continuous Eucharistic Intercession

I've been searching for an expression of Eucharistic offering that would continue the offering of the Mass throughout the day. How can I express my union with the eternal intercession that Jesus makes at the throne of the Father? How can I express my offering of the Body and Blood of Jesus in the moment to moment situation of daily living?

There are various beautiful, written expressions of such offerings; one is the morning offering in which we unite ourselves with all the Masses going on in the world; another is the chaplet of Divine Mercy (explained in another chapter).

My search was for a succinct expression that focused on the present need for intercession, which would also reflect the biblical expression of offering. What I discovered was a pattern in Sacred Scripture that has great meaning. In its simplest form it has three elements:

> *Father!*
> *Behold,*
> *Your Son.*

Father! All intercession and offering is ultimately directed to the Father. Jesus taught us to say "Father!" in the Lord's prayer. This is the way Jesus Himself prayed and interceded. This is the way Jesus offered Himself on the cross: *"Father, into Your hands, I commend My spirit"* (*Lk* 23:46). Only through the Holy Spirit can we cry, *"Abba, Father"* (see *Rom* 8:15).

Behold. It means to see and grasp the meaning of something. It means to see and understand. It calls for a response. Sometimes the Greek word is translated "lo" or "there." In this expression, it means to look at and respond with compassionate mercy.

51

Your Son. The Son of the Father, Jesus Christ, is *the* beloved
Son. He is the fullness of God's love and revelation.

The Father, looking upon His Son, will always have mercy.
His Son has reconciled us by His obedience, an obedience even
to death on the cross, and has opened the channel of God's infinite mercy to us.

This part of the expression takes various forms and can be
adapted to the given situation:

> Father, behold Your Son.
> Father, behold the Body of Your Son.
> Father, behold the broken Body of Your Son.
> Father, behold the Body of Your Son given for us.
> Father, behold the Blood of Your Son poured out for us.

This expression of "Father, behold Your Son" is the offering of
the whole Body of Christ, His Church. We are that Body, and so
we ask the Father to look upon us, the Body of His Son, and be
moved to have mercy on us in this very situation. Because of the
union with Jesus through the Spirit, we can and do approach the
Father in union with His Son. We ask the Father *to look* on us and
to see His Son. In the third Eucharistic prayer (Roman Rite) the
celebrant prays, "Father, . . . *look* with favor on Your Church's
offering, and *see* the Victim Whose death has reconciled us to
Yourself (emphasis added). "Father, look not on our sins, but on
the faith of Your Church, . . . " (Communion Rite).

We as a royal priesthood can continue this intercessory offering if we turn to the Father throughout the day and pray:
"Father, behold the Body of Your Son!" This is continuous
Eucharistic adoration and when we pray in this way we can
recall to mind the various occasions that express this Eucharistic
cry. When Mary responded to the Angel at the Annunciation she
said, *"Behold, I am the handmaid of the Lord"* (*Lk* 1:38, RSV)
and the word was made flesh—the first Eucharist! Jesus at that
moment also offered Himself to the Father—". . . *a body hast
Thou prepared for me; . . .'Lo, I have come to do Your will, O
God'"* (*Heb* 10:5,7, RSV)—Jesus virtually says, "Father, behold
Your Son!"

John the Baptist pointed out Jesus as the Eucharistic lamb—
"Behold, the lamb of God, Who takes away the sin of the world!"
(*Jn* 1:29, RSV).

We can hear this phrase echoed in the words of the Father at the baptism of Jesus, *"This is My beloved Son"* (*Mt* 3:17).

Then, on the cross, Jesus, seeing His mother and His beloved disciple (who represents us), said to His mother: *"Woman, behold, your Son!"* and then He said to the disciple, *"Behold your mother!"* (*Jn* 19:26-27, RSV). Here is Eucharist—here John is transformed from being merely the son of man to being the son of the Mother of God!

These transforming, Eucharistic words echo in our hearts. As Joseph of Arimathea and Nicodemus took down the Body of Jesus from the cross (see *Jn* 19:38-42) these words echoed in their hearts as they laid the Body of Jesus in the arms of His mother: "Woman, behold your SON!" At this moment of the "pieta" Mary renews her "yes" of the Annunciation, and echoing the words that opened her heart, she offers the Body of her Son to the Father:

Father, behold Your Son!

And now we continue to echo these words in each generation. Like Mary, we too can turn to the Father and offer Him His Son:

Father, behold Your Son!

In each and every situation of life we can offer to the Father the Body and Blood of His Son. In all joys and pains, in life and in death, we are members of the Body of the Son of God, and so Christ continues His life and death in us. In all circumstances and all places and at all times we can say:

Father, behold Your Son!
Father, behold the broken Body of Your Son!
Father, behold the Blood of Your Son poured out for us.

This way of offering the world around us is a way of living out the prayer of the Mass: "Father, . . . *look* with favor on Your Church's offering, and *see* the Victim Whose death has reconciled us to Yourself" (Eucharistic Prayer III).

This is Eucharistic intercession. This is asking the Father to look at our brokenness as the Body of Christ and see only His

Son. This is interceding with Jesus our High Priest for mercy; mercy on us and on the whole world.

Father, behold Your Son!

This is living Eucharistically. This is living as a royal priesthood.

Chapter 13

Chaplet of the Divine Mercy

The Chaplet of Divine Mercy is an intercessory prayer form that is explicitly Eucharistic. It consists of an offering of the Body and Blood of our Lord Jesus Christ to the Father—pleading mercy on us and on the whole world—not because we are worthy or in any way merit His mercy, but because of the infinite worth and merit of the passion of His Son.

It is prayed using the rosary beads, beginning with the Our Father, Hail Mary, and the Apostles' Creed. On the large beads is prayed:

> *Eternal Father, I offer You the Body and Blood, Soul and Divinity of Your dearly beloved Son, our Lord Jesus Christ in atonement for our sins and those of the whole world.*

On the small beads:

> *For the sake of His sorrowful passion, have mercy on us and on the whole world.*

The Chaplet is concluded with:

> *Holy God, Holy Mighty One, Holy Immortal One, have mercy on us and on the whole world* (from the *Diary* of Sr. Faustina, #475, 476).

The prayer is stark, simple and powerful. That has been my experience! I've come to pray this prayer at different times of the day as a Eucharistic prayer of intercession for a variety of needs, as part of the Stations of the cross, or as a novena prayer for intentions of special urgency. Phrases of the Chaplet keep recurring in my prayer and in my preaching.

What greater plea do we have for mercy than to offer the crucified and risen Body and Blood of our Lord Jesus? What greater need is there than atonement for our sins and those of the whole world? What a weight of sins—five billion sinners in the world! What a mountain of sins: injustices, hatreds, murders, abortions, jealousies, etc., etc.!

In the midst of this mountain of sin we can actually approach the throne of God, with no justice of our own. We approach the throne of mercy because of what Jesus has done for us and given to us. Jesus has by His passion, death, and resurrection revealed the Father's mercy and more than that, Jesus has given us a living memorial of His mercy in His Eucharistic Body and Blood.

So, by offering the Eucharistic Body and Blood of Jesus to the Father, we offer the one sacrifice that takes away the sins of the world. There is one obstacle to our salvation—SIN. The Blood of Jesus has taken away SIN, so *"their sins and their transgressions I will remember no more" (Heb* 10:17) becomes an expression of the New Covenant.

The offering of the chaplet of Divine Mercy is like a continual reminder to the Father of what Jesus did for us, namely that Jesus accepted a Body to do the perfect will of the Father, that is, to offer a perfect sacrifice. He sprinkled His own Blood on the mercy seat to cleanse us of our sins. So in the chaplet we remind the Father that we now have access to the throne of His mercy and can approach His throne with *"utter sincerity and absolute confidence" (Heb* 10:22).

In the chaplet we remind ourselves of what has been given us—mercy; mercy on us and on the whole world. We remind ourselves of Jesus and His gift.

In the chaplet we intercede with the power of the Eucharist Itself as we extend the Eucharistic offering of the Body and Blood, Soul and Divinity of the dearly beloved Son of the Father, our Lord Jesus Christ to each moment.

In the chaplet we truly intercede as a priestly people because we intercede for the needs of the whole world and not just for our own personal needs. We intercede as the Body of Christ, concerned for the whole Body of Christ, His Church. We intercede as the "universal sacrament of salvation" (*Lumen Gentium*, #48), asking for mercy on the whole world.

In the chaplet we worship the thrice-holy God. "Holy God, Holy Mighty One, Holy Immortal One!" We turn to the God of infinite mercy to "have mercy on us and on the whole world."

In the chaplet we virtually ask the Father not to look on this sinful world except through the wounds of His crucified Son. So in seeing us, the Father will see His Son.

And for that we pray: "For the sake of His sorrowful passion, have mercy on us and on the whole world."

Our Lord revealed to Sister Faustina that He wanted her to pray this chaplet of Divine Mercy without ceasing (from the *Diary* of Sr. Faustina, #687). More information on the devotion to the Divine Mercy can be obtained from the Marian Helpers, Stockbridge, MA 01263.

Chapter 14

The Rosary is a Prayer of Intercession

The Rosary is a prayer of intercession that has been given the highest recommendation by many popes.

Pope Paul VI in his apostolic exhortation, *Marialis Cultus,* in focusing on the Rosary, recalls Pope Pius XII's description of it as "the compendium of the Gospel" that fosters contemplative prayer. He points out that research has brought out that it is inspired by the Gospel and is a Gospel prayer of the redemptive incarnation. Its orientation is the praise of Jesus, Son of God and Son of Mary. Its composition is praise, petition and contemplation—calling for a quiet rhythm and a lingering pace—with a warp of Aves and a woof of mysteries.

Pope Paul points out that the Rosary is not liturgy but it is not in opposition to it. The liturgy is continued in the Rosary like an echo. The Rosary, in turn, draws its force from the liturgy, leads back to it and prepares for it. The Rosary contemplates the mysteries that the liturgy exercises in sign. Like the liturgy it is based on Sacred Scripture, it is communal, and it is focused on the mysteries of Christ.

Father Frederick Jelly, O.P. extends this relationship of the liturgy and the Rosary. He points out that the three Mysteries of the Rosary echo the Eucharist and prepare for it: The Joyful Mysteries contemplate the real *presence* of the Lord, the Sorrowful Mysteries resonate with the *sacrifice* of the Lord, and the Glorious Mysteries celebrate the *communion* of God and man (*Bulletin of Christian Affairs* #66, Oct., 1976). The Rosary is a Eucharistic prayer of intercession.

The point that Father Jelly makes about the relation of the Rosary and the Eucharist I find very rich, especially since he chooses the three dimensions of the Eucharist as presence, sacrifice, and communion. Pope John Paul II in his encyclical *Redeemer of Man,* describes the Eucharist with these same three dimensions: "It is at one and the same time a Sacrifice-Sacrament, a Communion-Sacrament, and a Presence-Sacrament." These three dimensions of the Eucharist also reveal some of the grandeur of its mystery. When we contemplate the Mysteries of the Rosary we enter into some of this mystery.

When we contemplate the Joyful Mysteries of the Rosary, for example, we enter into the *presence* of the Lord in His humanity: announced and conceived in the womb of Mary, coming in visitation to bring the Holy Spirit to Elizabeth and John the Baptist, present to us as a newborn child, offered in His humanity to the Father and then found in the temple about His Father's priorities yet subjecting Himself to Mary and Joseph. When we contemplate the agony of Jesus in the garden, at the scourging, being crowned with thorns, carrying His cross to Calvary, and finally crucified, we enter into His *sacrifice* of His total gift of Himself in love and in obedience to the Father's will. Then when we contemplate the Glorious Mysteries of Christ's Resurrection, Ascension into heaven, the sending of the Holy Spirit, the Assumption, and crowning of Mary as Queen, we enter into a mystical *communion* with the heavenly mysteries in store for us as members of the Body of Christ. We, too, like Mary, are to rise with Him, ascend and reign with Him by the power of the Holy Spirit.

Pope John Paul II, in three short talks in 1981, gave his personal testimony to the power of the Rosary. He exhorts us to use it as intercessory prayer. Let these exhortations stand next to the request of our Blessed Mother made at Lourdes and Fatima that we pray the Rosary daily, that we intercede daily for all of "us sinners, now and at the hour of our death." I quote here from those three testimonies of the Holy Pontiff:

John Paul II—Summary of the Whole Gospel

I address my affectionate and cordial greeting to all of you gathered here to recite with me the Angelus, a prayer that synthesizes, in a brief but effective way, the Mystery of the Incarnation.

As you know, tomorrow begins the month of October, which the piety of Christians has wished to connect, in particular, to a more committed and devout daily recitation of the Holy Rosary, which my predecessors, Pius XII and Paul VI, wished to call "the summary of the whole Gospel." For centuries this prayer has had a privileged place in devotion to the Blessed Virgin, "under whose protection the praying faithful seek refuge in all dangers and necessities" (*Lumen Gentium,* 66).

The Rosary is at the same time a simple prayer, but theologically rich in biblical references. For this reason Christians love it and recite it with frequency and with fervor, well aware of its authentic "Gospel Inspiration," of which Paul VI speaks in his apostolic exhortation on devotion to the Blessed Virgin.

In the Rosary we meditate on the principal salvific events that were accomplished in Christ; from the virginal conception to the culminating moments of Easter and the glorification of the Mother of God. This prayer is one of praise and a continued plea to Mary Most Holy, that she may intercede for us poor sinners at every moment of our day, to the hour of our death.

I wish therefore to exhort you to rediscover and value ever more, in the month of October, the Holy Rosary as a personal and family prayer addressed to her who is the mother of the individual faithful and Mother of the Church.

In support of this exhortation of mine, I heartily impart the Apostolic Blessing.

L'Osservatore Romano
September 30, 1981

John Paul II—*I am Indebted*

And again I have become indebted to the Blessed Virgin and to all the Patron Saints. Could I forget that the event in St. Peter's Square took place on the day and at the hour when the first appearance of the Mother of Christ to the poor little peasants has been remembered for over sixty years at Fatima in Portugal? For, in everything that happened to me on that very day, I felt that extraordinary motherly protection and care, which turned out to be stronger than the deadly bullet.

Today is the memorial of Our Lady of the Holy Rosary. The whole month of October is the Month of the Rosary. Now that nearly five months later it has been granted me to meet you again at the Wednesday audience, dear brothers and sisters, I want these first words that I address to you to be words of gratitude, love and deep trust, just as the Holy Rosary is and always remains a prayer of gratitude, love and trustful request: the prayer of the Mother of the Church.

And I once again encourage and invite you all to this prayer, especially during this Month of the Rosary.

L'Osservatore Romano
October 12, 1981

John Paul II's Rosary

It is our Prayer

The Rosary is my favorite prayer. A marvelous prayer. Marvelous in its simplicity and its depth. In this prayer we repeat many times the words that the Virgin Mary heard from the Archangel and from her cousin Elizabeth. This whole Church joins in these words. It can be said that the Rosary is, in a way, a prayer-comment on the last chapter of the Constitution *"Lumen Gentium"* of Vatican II, the chapter that deals with "the rose of the Blessed Virgin Mary, Mother of God, in the mystery of Christ and the Church."

It is the Life of Christ

Against the background of the words "Ave Maria" there pass before the eyes of the soul the principal events of the life of Jesus Christ. They are composed of the Joyful, Sorrowful and Glorious Mysteries, and they put us in living communion with Jesus through, we could say, the Heart of His Mother.

It is our Life

Our heart can enclose in these decades of the Rosary all the facts that make up the life of the individual, the family, the nation, the Church and mankind: personal matters and those close to us and, in particular, those of the persons closest to us, our dear ones. In this way the simple prayer of the Rosary beats out the rhythm of human life.

It is our Thanks

In the last few weeks I have had numerous proofs of kindness on the part of people all over the world. I want to express my gratitude in decades of the Rosary. In order to be able to express it in prayer, as well as in a human way; in the prayer, so simple and so rich, that the Rosary is. I cordially exhort everyone to recite it.

L'Osservatore Romano
October 26, 1981

Chapter 15

Intercession is a Way of Life

Intercession is a way of life. It becomes a way of living out what St. Peter described as "offering spiritual sacrifices":

> *You too are living stones, built as an edifice of spirit, into a holy priest-hood, offering spiritual sacrifices acceptable to God through Jesus Christ* (*1 Pet* 2:5).

The offering of these spiritual sacrifices are expressed in various ways:

- as a prayer of praise (see *Heb* 13:15), of thanks (see *Ps* 50:23), of contrition (see *Ps* 51:19), of petition (see *Heb* 5:7);

- as a life of good deeds and generosity (see *Heb* 13:16), offering our bodies as a living sacrifice holy and acceptable to God (see *Rom* 12:1);

- and above all in the Eucharist as we unite ourselves with Christ in the "breaking of the bread" for the forgiveness of sins.

To offer gifts and sacrifices for sins is really the very nature of the priesthood and of intercession. Personally, I am moving toward identifying a life of intercession with "offering spiritual sacrifices," which means growing in holiness. To sacrifice is to cleanse, to make holy, and to make a spiritual sacrifice is to make holy by offering *ourselves* in communion with the Holy Spirit. It is not a sacrifice of animals or food offered as a sign of ourselves, as in the Old Testament, but rather it is a total gift of our very selves. It is to be Eucharistic.

The key issue in living such a life of intercession is *holiness* because offering spiritual sacrifices demands holiness. Yet holiness all too often scares priests, religious, and people. Unfortunately, a mistaken notion of holiness is so deeply ingrained in us that we shy away from it and thereby hinder our work of intercession.

Holiness is not a reward for a good life or for things well done—it is the presence of another person within us. Holiness is the presence and the power of the person of the Lord Jesus Christ through the working of the Holy Spirit. Holiness is being "possessed and led by the Spirit" (Paul VI, *Evangelii Nuntiandi,* 75).

Holiness has to do more with the content of the vessel and less with the worthiness of the vessel. The indwelling of the Holy Spirit will transform our vessels of clay into His vessels for the kingdom. The first and continuing step in holiness is to ask for it: ask for His Holy Spirit to fill your heart. It is this holiness that ushers in the kingdom.

> *"Seek first His kingship over you, His way of holiness, and all these things will be given you besides"* (*Mt* 6:33).

To live a life of intercession, then, means to live a life surrendered to the Holy Spirit, yielding to Him our hearts, our minds, our wills in order that He might use us for the establishment of the kingdom. Pope Paul put it this way:

"In the pursuit of perfect charity which guides your existence, what attitude could you have other than a total surrender to the Holy Spirit Who, working in the Church, calls you to the freedom of the sons of God?" (*Evangelica Testifiatio,* 6).

The life of intercession is also summed up in the words of St. Paul to the Church of Thessalonica. His words have been a kind of theme over the years that serve to remind me of God's will:

> *Rejoice always, never cease praying, render constant thanks; such is God's will for you in Christ Jesus* (*1 Thes* 5:16-18).

To live a life of intercession is to live Eucharistically.

Chapter 16

The Need for United Intercession

It seems to me that the Father is waiting for the whole Church, Head and Body, to ask for, to intercede for, the coming of the kingdom. He is waiting for the Church to cooperate in His plan. Is the delay of the full coming of His kingdom due to our lack of asking in an effective way? Is the Church unable to hasten the Day of the Lord (see *2 Pet* 3:12) (the full coming of His kingdom) because she is failing to ask in a conscious and *united* intercession? To me this means that if the Church, both priests and people, with one heart and one mind in Christ ask in a conscious, fully aware plea for the Holy Spirit, then the Day of the Lord will indeed be hastened.

There are a host of obstacles to this kind of effective asking, but the most basic of them is the lack of unity of heart and mind in Christ. Where among us are the two or three who are so fully agreed in their hearts and minds and so united in Christ Jesus that whatever they ask for will be granted to them by the Father in Heaven? The basic differences of our philosophies, cosmologies, theologies and faith are enough to keep us separated; not to mention the resentments, jealousies, doubts, negative thoughts, ignorance and indifference.

It seems to me that the Father is patiently waiting for His Church to ask for the coming of His kingdom—in a united way. How long will the Father need to wait for this united plea?

Intercession is necessary for hastening the coming of the kingdom. And the more I intercede, the more I am becoming conscious of the need of unity among us both in heart and mind. And yet, my personal experience is that the more I intercede, the more inadequate I feel because of lack of unity and my own weakness, sinfulness and failure. What a happy fault! I can no longer rely on my own strength, but can only ask out of weakness, "Come, Lord Jesus."

Who among us has heard the call to a united intercession for the coming of the kingdom? Are there some among us who are willing to die the martyr's death daily to become one heart and one mind in Christ and implore the Spirit? Who is willing to submit to another so as to become one in heart and mind? We have the model of the Trinity itself to teach us about submission. The Divine Persons are totally submissive to One Another in unity. What greater revelation of the mystery of the Trinity than Jesus submitting to the Father on the cross?

It is this kind of unity that Jesus prayed for at the Last Supper so that the world would both believe and know that Jesus was the one sent from the Father. We need to intercede with this same kind of unity for the kingdom to come and so fulfill the prayer of Jesus.

St. Paul pleaded with the Christian community for this kind of unity (see *Phil* 2:1-4), especially in the celebration of the Eucharist (see *1 Cor* 11:17-34), because he knew united intercession is needed for the coming of the Kingdom of God.

Why do we need to intercede? So that the kingdom may come. God is waiting for our united cooperation.

Appendix I

Interceding for Priests

Prayers for priests? Yes, priests need prayers as well or even more than others. We are human and we are sinners, and we need the prayer support of the faithful. As shepherds of the people, we come under a special attack of Satan and his temptations; we too are in the world and can all too easily become "of the world."

During the years of Bethany House of Intercession (a community of priests interceding for brother priests into which priests could come and join in on the daily intercession), we were supported by the intercession of hundreds of lay associates and priests who prayed with us. This ministry of intercession is continued by the *Fraternity of Priests* and also needs the prayer support of the faithful.

The *Fraternity of Priests* is associated with the Franciscan University of Steubenville, Steubenville, OH 43952, and is fostering gatherings of priests, especially as a follow-up for the conferences held for priests over the past years at the University. The intention is to foster deeper conversion to Christ and renewal in the Spirit. Your prayer support is needed.

One form of prayer for priests used at Bethany House of Intercession was a prayer adapted from *Ephesians* 3:14-21. We made it available to all who wanted to be associated with us. I offer it here:

Prayer for our Shepherds

Father, we kneel before You, from Whom every family in Heaven and on earth takes its name; and we pray that You will bestow on priests gifts in keeping with the riches of Your glory. May You strengthen them inwardly through the working of Your Spirit. May Christ dwell in their hearts through faith, and may

66

charity be the root and foundation of their lives. Thus they will be able to grasp fully, with all the holy ones, the breadth and length and height and depth of Christ's love, and experience this love which surpasses all knowledge, so that they may attain to Your fullness, O God. To You Whose power now at work in them can do immeasurably more than we can ask or imagine, to You be glory in the Church and in Christ Jesus through all generations, world without end. Amen.

Bethany House of Intercession

The Emmaus Spirituality Program is a renewal program for priests. They present the following prayer:

Prayer for Priests

Lord Jesus, hear our prayer
for the spiritual renewal of priests.
We praise You for giving their ministry to the Church.
In these days, renew them with the gifts of Your Spirit.

You once opened the Scriptures
to the disciples on the road to Emmaus.
Now renew Your ordained ministers
with the truth and power of Your Word.

In the Eucharist You gave the Emmaus disciples
renewed life and hope.
Nourish priests with Your own Body and Blood.
Help them to imitate in their lives
the death and resurrection they celebrate at Your altar.

Give priests enthusiasm for the Gospel,
zeal for the salvation of mankind,
courage in leadership,
humility in service,
fraternity with one another
and with all their brothers and sisters in You.

For You love them, Lord Jesus,
and we love and pray for them in Your name. Amen.

Appendix II

Church Statement on Intercession

Second Vatican Council

In the *Constitution on the Sacred Liturgy* (*Sacrosanctum Concilium* #53), the Church fathers restored the ancient "Bidding Prayers" as an official part of the Mass, and also the Liturgy of the Hours. They offer another chance for the faithful to participate actively:

> Especially on Sundays and feasts of obligation, there is to be restored, after the Gospel and the homily, "the common prayer" or "the prayer of the faithful." By this prayer, in which the people are to take part, intercession will be made for holy Church, for the civil authorities, for those oppressed by various needs, for all mankind, and for the salvation of the entire world (cf. *1 Tim* 2:1-2).

The Catechism of the Catholic Church

In the Old Testament, the intercession of Moses is described as a powerful example of mediation for the people of Israel, as well as the intercessory prayer of King David and the prophet Elijah (see #2578 to 2584).

Moses and the prayer of the mediator (#2574 to 2577)

> Once the promise begins to be fulfilled (Passover, the Exodus, the gift of the Law, and the ratification of the covenant), the prayer of Moses becomes the most striking example of intercessory prayer, which will be fulfilled in "the one mediator between God and men, the man Christ Jesus."

Here again the initiative is God's. From the midst of the burning bush he calls Moses. This event will remain one of the primordial images of prayer in the spiritual tradition of Jews and Christians alike. When "the God of Abraham, of Isaac, and of Jacob" calls Moses to be his servant, it is because he is the living God who wants men to live. God reveals himself in order to save them, though he does not do this alone or despite them: he calls Moses to be his messenger, an associate in his compassion, his work of salvation. There is something of a divine plea in this mission, and only after long debate does Moses attune his own will to that of the Savior God. But in the dialogue in which God confides in him, Moses also learns how to pray: he balks, makes excuses, above all questions: and it is in response to his question that the Lord confides his ineffable name, which will be revealed through his mighty deeds.

"Thus the Lord used to speak to Moses face to face, as a man speaks to his friend." Moses' prayer is characteristic of contemplative prayer by which God's servant remains faithful to his mission. Moses converses with God often and at length, climbing the mountain to hear and entreat him and coming down to the people to repeat the words of his God for their guidance. Moses "is entrusted with all my house. With him I speak face to face, clearly, not in riddles," for "Moses was very humble, more so than anyone else on the face of the earth."

From this intimacy with the faithful God, slow to anger and abounding in steadfast love, Moses drew strength and determination for his intercession. He does not pray for himself but for the people whom God made his own. Moses already intercedes for them during the battle with the Amalekites and prays to obtain healing for Miriam. But it is chiefly after their apostasy that Moses "stands in the breach" before God in order to save the people. The arguments of his prayer—for intercession is also a mysterious battle—

will inspire boldness of the great intercessors among the Jewish people and in the Church: God is love; he is therefore righteous and faithful; he cannot contradict himself; he must remember his marvellous deeds, since his glory is at stake, and he cannot forsake this people that bears his name.

In the New Testament, we have the example of Jesus and St. Paul teaching us to intercede:

Prayer of Intercession (#2634 to 2636)

Intercession is a prayer of petition which leads us to pray as Jesus did. He is the one intercessor with the Father on behalf of all men, especially sinners. He is "able for all time to save those who draw near to God through him, since he always lives to make intercession for them." The Holy Spirit "himself intercedes for us . . . and intercedes for the saints according to the will of God."

Since Abraham, intercession—asking on behalf of another—has been characteristic of a heart attuned to God's mercy. In the age of the Church, Christian intercession participates in Christ's, as an expression of the communion of saints. In intercession, he who prays looks "not only to his own interests, but also to the interests of others," even to the point of praying for those who do him harm.

The first Christian communities lived this form of fellowship intensely. Thus the Apostle Paul gives them a share in his ministry of preaching the Gospel but also intercedes for them. The intercession of Christians recognizes no boundaries: "for all men, for kings and all who are in high positions," for persecutors, for the salvation of those who reject the Gospel.

Eucharistic Intercession (#2643)

The Eucharist contains and expresses all forms of

prayer: it is "the pure offering" of the whole Body of Christ to the glory of God's name and, according to the traditions of East and West, it is *the* "sacrifice of praise."

Rich in Mercy

In his encyclical on Divine Mercy, John Paul II concludes the final chapter with a powerful summons to the Church to intercede for Divine Mercy:

The Church Appeals to the Mercy of God

The Church proclaims the truth about God's mercy which is made known in the crucified and risen Christ and she makes it known in various ways. The Church also tries to be merciful to people through people because she considers this to be an indispensable condition for a better, "more human" world, today and tomorrow.

And yet at no time and in no period of history—especially at a turning point like ours—can the Church forget about *prayer, which is a cry for the mercy of God* in the midst of the many forms of evil that weigh upon mankind and threaten it. This imploring of mercy is precisely the fundamental right and at the same time the duty of the Church in Christ Jesus. It is the right and duty of the church toward God and at the same time toward humanity.

The more the human conscience succumbs to secularization and loses its sense of the very meaning of the word "mercy," the more it moves away from God and the mystery of mercy. Therefore *the Church has all the more the right and the duty* to appeal to God's mercy with "loud cries" (*Heb* 5:7). Such "loud cries" ought to be the cry of the Church of our times to God for mercy as she announces and proclaims the certainty of that mercy in the crucified and risen Christ, that is, the Paschal Mystery. This mystery carries within itself the fullest revelation of mercy, namely, that love is more powerful than death, more powerful than sin and every evil, that love lifts man from his deepest falls and frees him from his greatest threats.

Modern man feels these threats. What has been said on this point is only a beginning. Modern man often asks about the solutions of these terrible tensions which have built up in the world between peoples. And if at times he *lacks the courage to utter this word "mercy,"* or if his conscience is empty of religious content and he does not find the equivalent, so much the greater is the *necessity for the Church to utter this word,* not only in her own name but also in the name of all people of our time.

It is necessary that everything that I have said in this present letter on mercy *be continuously changed and transformed into an ardent prayer:* into a cry for mercy on the people of the modern world with all their needs and threats. *May this cry be filled with that truth about mercy* which has found such rich expression in the Sacred Scriptures, in Tradition, and in the authentic life of faith of countless generations of the People of God. Like the sacred writers let us cry out to God who cannot despise anything that He has made, (*Gen* 1:31; *Ps* 145;9; *Wis* 11:24), Him who is faithful to Himself, His fatherhood and His love. And like the prophets, let us appeal to that love which has maternal characteristics—and, like a mother, goes after each of her children, after each lost sheep, even if the lost are in the millions, even if the evil in the world outweighs honesty, even if mankind deserves, because of its sins, a kind of modern "flood," as did the generation of Noah.

Let us appeal also to that kind of fatherly love revealed to us by Christ in His messianic mission, which reached its ultimate expression in His cross, in His death and in His resurrection! Let us appeal to God through Christ, mindful of the words of Mary's *Magnificat* which proclaims "mercy from age to age."

Let us cry out for God's own mercy for this present generation! May the Church, which like Mary continues to be the spiritual mother of humankind, express in this prayer her total maternal concern, as well as that trusting love from which is born the most burning need for prayer.

Let us cry out, guided by that faith, hope and love that Christ grafted in our hearts. This cry for mercy is at the same time an expression of our love of God, from whom modern man has distanced himself and made of Him a stranger, proclaiming in various ways that he doesn't "need" God. This then is mercy, the love of God whose insult—rejection by modern man—we feel deeply and are ready to cry out with Christ on the cross, "Father, forgive them, for they do not know what they do" (*Lk* 23:34 RSV).

This cry for mercy is at the same time *love for all of mankind*. Mercy is love for all peoples without exception or division: without difference of race, culture, language, or world-view, without distinction between friends and enemies. This cry for mercy is love for all people. Mercy desires every true good for each individual and for every human community, for every family, for every nation, for every social group, for youth, adults, parents, and for the elderly and the sick. It is love for everyone, without exception or division. This cry for mercy is love for all people, the care which ensures for everyone all true good, and removes and drives away every sort of evil.

And if any of our contemporaries do not share the faith and hope which bid me, as a servant of the mysteries of God (cf. *1 Cor* 1:1), to implore the mercy of God Himself for mankind in this hour of history, *then may they understand the reason for my concern. It is dictated by love* for mankind, for all that is human and which, according to the intuitions of many of our contemporaries, is threatened by an immense danger.

The same mystery of Christ, which reveals to us the great vocations of mankind, which obliged me to proclaim in the Encyclical *Redemptor Hominis* mankind's incomparable dignity, also obliges me to announce mercy as God's merciful love revealed in that same mystery of Christ. This mystery of Christ also obliges me to appeal to this mercy and implore this mercy on our difficult and critical times of the Church and of the world as we approach the end of the second millennium.

In the name of Jesus Christ crucified and risen from the dead, in the spirit of His messianic mission, which endures in the works of mankind, *we lift up our voice and plead:* that the love which is in the Father, may once again be revealed at this stage of history; and that, through the work of the Son and the Holy Spirit, this love which is in the Father, may be once again shown to be present in our modern world as more powerful than evil and more powerful than sin and death. We plead this through the intercession of Mary, who does not cease to proclaim "mercy . . . from generation to generation," and also through the intercession of the saints in whom have been completely fulfilled the words of the Sermon on the Mount: "Blessed are the merciful, for they shall obtain mercy: (*Mt* 5:7).

It is not permissible for the Church, for any reason to withdraw into herself as she continues the great task of implementing the Second Vatican Council. In this implementing we can rightly see a new phase of the self-realization of the Church—in keeping with the age in which it has been our destiny to live. *The reason for her existence* is, in fact, to reveal God, that the Father who allows us to "see" Himself in Christ (cf. *Jn* 14:9). No matter how strong the resistance of human history may be, no matter how estranged the civilization of the world, no matter how great the denial of God in the human world, so much the greater must be our closeness to that mystery which, hidden for centuries in God, was then truly shared with man, in time, through Jesus Christ.

With my Apostolic Blessing.

Given in Rome, at St. Peter's, on the thirtieth day of November, the First Sunday of Advent, in the year 1980, the Third of my Pontificate.

John Paul II, Pope

(Re-translated from the original Polish and the official Latin texts by Rev. George W. Kosicki, CSB.)

Appendix III

Two Sample Formulas for the General Intercessions at Mass

1. Introduction

**My brothers and sisters,
we are gathered to celebrate the mystery
of our salvation in Jesus Christ.
Let us ask God our Father
to open for all the world this fountain of life and
blessing.**

Intercessions led by the deacon or other minister

A. **For all who have dedicated themselves to God,
that He will help them to be faithful to their promise,
we pray to the Lord:** R. *Lord hear our prayer.*

B. **For peace among nations,
that God may rid the world of violence,
and let us serve Him in freedom,
we pray to the Lord:** R. *Lord hear our prayer.*

C. **For the aged who suffer from loneliness and infirmity,
that we will sustain them by our love,
we pray to the Lord:** R. *Lord hear our prayer.*

D. **For all of us gathered here,
that God will teach us to use wisely**

**the good things He has given us,
that they will lead us closer to Him
and to the eternal blessings He promises,
we pray to the Lord:** R. *Lord hear our prayer.*

Concluding prayer by the priest

> **Father,
> hear the prayers of Your people.
> Give us what You have inspired us
> to ask You for in faith.
> We ask this through Christ our Lord.** R. *Amen.*

2. Introduction

> **Gathered together in Christ
> As brothers and sisters,
> let us call to mind God's many blessings
> and ask Him to hear the prayers
> which He Himself inspires us to ask.**

Intercessions led by the deacon or other minister

A. **For our Pope N., our Bishop N., all the Church's
   ministers and the people they have been called to lead
   and serve, we pray to the Lord:** R. *Lord hear our prayer.*

B. **For those who serve us in public office
   and for all those entrusted with the common good,
   we pray to the Lord:** R. *Lord hear our prayer.*

C. **For all travelers, by land, air, or sea;
   for prisoners; and for those unjustly deprived
   of freedom, we pray to the Lord:** R. *Lord hear our prayer.*

Concluding prayer by the priest

> **Father,**
> **hear the prayers of Your Church.**
> **In Your love,**
> **make up for what is lacking in our faith.**
> **We ask this through Christ our Lord.** R. *Amen.*

Intercessory Prayers of Good Friday

I. For the Church

> **Let us pray, dear friends,**
> **for the holy Church of God throughout the world,**
> **that God the almighty Father guide it and gather it**
> **together so that we may worship Him**
> **in peace and tranquility.**

Silent prayer. Then the priest sings or says:

> **Almighty and eternal God,**
> **You have shown Your glory to all nations**
>   **in Christ, Your Son.**
> **Guide the work of Your Church.**
> **Help it to persevere in faith, proclaim Your name,**
> **and bring Your salvation to people everywhere.**
>
> **We ask this through Christ our Lord.** R. *Amen.*

II. For the Pope

> **Let us pray for our Holy Father, Pope N.,**
> **that God Who chose him to be bishop**
> **may give him health and strength**
> **to guide and govern God's holy people.**

Silent prayer. Then the priest sings or says:

Almighty and eternal God,
You guide all things by Your word,
You govern all Christian people.
In Your love protect the Pope You have
  chosen for us.
Under his leadership deepen our faith
and make us better Christians.

We ask this through Christ our Lord. R. *Amen.*

III. For the clergy and laity of the Church

Let us pray
for N., our bishop,
for all bishops, priests, and deacons;
for all who have a special ministry in the Church
and for all God's people.

Silent prayer. Then the priest sings or says:

Almighty and eternal God,
Your Spirit guides the Church
and makes it holy.
Listen to our prayers
and help each of us
in his own vocation
to do Your work more faithfully.

We ask this through Christ our Lord. R. *Amen.*

IV. For those preparing for baptism

Let us pray
for those [among us] preparing for baptism,
that God in His mercy
make them responsive to His love,
forgive their sins through the water of new birth,
and give them life in Jesus Christ our Lord.

Silent prayer. Then the priest sings or says:

> **Almighty and eternal God,**
> **You continually bless Your Church with new**
> **members.**
> **Increase the faith and understanding**
> **of those [among us] preparing for baptism.**
> **Give them a new birth in these living waters**
> **and make them members of Your chosen family.**
>
> **We ask this through Christ our Lord.** R. *Amen.*

V. For the unity of Christians

> **Let us pray**
> **for all our brothers and sisters**
> **who share our faith in Jesus Christ,**
> **that God may gather and keep together in one**
> **Church**
> **all those who seek the truth with sincerity.**

Silent prayer. Then the priest sings or says:

> **Almighty and eternal God,**
> **You keep together those You have united.**
> **Look kindly on all who follow Jesus Your Son.**
> **We are all consecrated to You by our common**
> **baptism.**
> **Make us one in the fullness of faith,**
> **and keep us one in the fellowship of love.**
>
> **We ask this through Christ our Lord.** R. *Amen.*

VI. For the Jewish people

**Let us pray
for the Jewish people,
the first to hear the word of God,
that they may continue to grow in the love of
His name
and in faithfulness to His covenant.**

Silent prayer. Then the priest sings or says:

**Almighty and eternal God,
long ago You gave Your promise to Abraham
and his posterity.
Listen to Your Church as we pray
that the people You first made Your own
may arrive at the fullness of redemption.**

We ask this through Christ our Lord. R. *Amen.*

VII. For those who do not believe in Christ

**Let us pray
for those who do not believe in Christ,
that the light of the Holy Spirit
may show them the way to salvation.**

Silent prayer. Then the priest sings or says:

**Almighty and eternal God,
enable those who do not acknowledge Christ
to find the truth
as they walk before You in sincerity of heart.
Help us to grow in love for one another,
to grasp more fully the mystery of Your godhead,
and to become more perfect witnesses of Your love
in the sight of men.**

We ask this through Christ our Lord. R. *Amen.*

VIII. For those who do not believe in God

**Let us pray
for those who do not believe in God,
that they may find Him
by sincerely following all that is right.**

Silent prayer. Then the priest sings or says:

**Almighty and eternal God,
You created mankind
so that all might long to find You
and have peace when You are found.
Grant that, in spite of the hurtful things
that stand in their way,
they may all recognize in the lives of Christians
the tokens of Your love and mercy,
and gladly acknowledge You
as the one true God and Father of us all.**

We ask this through Christ our Lord. R. *Amen.*

IX. For all in public office

**Let us pray
for those who serve us in public office,
that God may guide their minds and hearts,
so that all men may live in true peace
       and freedom.**

Silent prayer. Then the priest sings or says:

**Almighty and eternal God,
You know the longings of men's hearts
and You protect their rights.
In Your goodness
watch over those in authority,
so that people everywhere may enjoy
religious freedom, security, and peace.**

We ask this through Christ our Lord. R. *Amen.*

X. For those in special need

Let us pray, dear friends,
that God the almighty Father
may heal the sick,
comfort the dying,
give safety to travelers,
free those unjustly deprived of liberty,
and rid the world of falsehood,
hunger, and disease.

Silent prayer. Then the priest sings or says:

Almighty, ever-living God,
You give strength to the weary
and new courage to those who have lost heart.
Hear the prayers of all who call on You in any trouble
that they may have the joy of receiving Your help
in their need.

We ask this through Christ our Lord. R. *Amen.*

A NOVENA OF INTERCESSIONS FOR PENTECOST

Ascension Thursday

In joy of spirit let us acclaim Christ, Who sits at the right hand of the Father.
R. *Lord Jesus, You are the King of glory.*

King of glory, You took with You our frail humanity to be glorified in Heaven; remove the sins of the world, and restore us to the innocence which was ours before the Fall.
R. *Lord Jesus, You are the King of glory.*

You came down from Heaven on a pilgrimage of love; grant that we may take the same path to Your presence.
R. *Lord Jesus, You are the King of glory.*

You promised to draw all things to Yourself; do not allow any one of us to be separated from Your Body.
R. *Lord Jesus, You are the King of glory.*

Where You have gone before us in glory, may we follow You in mind and heart.
R. *Lord Jesus, You are the King of glory.*

True God, we await Your coming as our judge; may we see the vision of Your glory and Your mercy in company with all the dead.
R. *Lord Jesus, You are the King of glory.*

Friday

All praise and glory to Christ, Who promised that the power of the Holy Spirit would come down on the apostles. Let us cry out:
R. *Send forth Your light and Your truth.*

Jesus, word of truth, wisdom and splendor of the Father,
send forth
Your light and Your truth, that our words and deeds today
may bear witness to You before our brothers and sisters.
R. *Send forth Your light and Your truth.*

May we always understand and savor the things of the
Spirit, so as not to fall into sin but enter into life and peace.
R. *Send forth Your light and Your truth.*

May Your Spirit help us in our weakness, that we may know
how to pray as we ought.
R. *Send forth Your light and Your truth.*

Fill us with love and all knowledge, that we may instruct and
correct one another.
R. *Send forth Your light and Your truth.*

Saturday

Let us bless Christ, on Whom the Holy Spirit came down in
the form of a dove. Let us pray to Him, and seal our prayer
by saying:
R. *Amen.*

Lord, send the Spirit of Your promise, that Your Church
may be continually renewed in life and vigor.
R. *Amen.*

May all peoples acclaim You as king and God; may Israel
become Your prized possession.
R. *Amen.*

You cast out devils; cast out from us all scandal and
stubborn pride.
R. *Amen.*

At Pentecost You undid the disunity of Babel; by Your Spirit gather all in unity, and spread the one faith throughout the world.
R. *Amen.*

May Your Spirit dwell within us, and raise to life our mortal bodies.
R. *Amen.*

Sunday

We do not know how to pray as we ought, but the Spirit Himself prays for us with inexpressible longing. Let us then say:
R. *May the Holy Spirit pray on our behalf.*

Lord Jesus, shepherd in glory, give wisdom and counsel to our shepherds, to lead Your flock more surely to salvation.
R. *May the Holy Spirit pray on our behalf.*

You are exalted in Heaven, and are rich in mercy; look with compassion on the poor and needy on earth.
R. *May the Holy Spirit pray on our behalf.*

You were conceived by the Virgin Mary by the overshadowing of the Holy Spirit; sustain those vowed to virginity in the spirit of their self-offering.
R. *May the Holy Spirit pray on our behalf.*

You are our priest, offering praise to the Father in the Holy Spirit; unite all mankind in Your sacrifice of praise.
R. *May the Holy Spirit pray on our behalf.*

May the dead enter into the glorious freedom of God's children, and the fullness of redemption for their bodies.
R. *May the Holy Spirit pray on our behalf.*

Monday

Let us give thanks to Christ, Who filled the apostles and the whole Church with the consolation of the Holy Spirit. In union with all the faithful, let us cry out:
R. *Lord, send Your consoling Spirit into Your Church.*

Lord Jesus, mediator between God and men, You chose priests to share Your work; through them may all rise with You to the Father.
R. *Lord, send Your consoling Spirit into Your Church.*

Grant that rich and poor may meet in friendship, for You are the God of both; do not let the rich make riches their god.
R. *Lord, send Your consoling Spirit into Your Church.*

**Make Your Gospel known to all peoples;
that all may come to obey You in faith.**
R. *Lord, send Your consoling Spirit into Your Church.*

**Send forth Your Spirit, gentlest of consolers,
to wipe away the tears of all who mourn.**
R. *Lord, send Your consoling Spirit into Your Church.*

Purify the souls of the departed, and receive them into the company of Your saints and chosen ones in Heaven.
R. *Lord, send Your consoling Spirit into Your Church.*

Tuesday

All honor and glory to Christ, Who has given the faithful a share in the Holy Spirit. Let us cry out to Him, saying:
R. *Christ, hear us.*

Send forth the Holy Spirit from the Father, to cleanse and strengthen the Church and spread it throughout the world.
R. *Christ, hear us.*

Lord, by Your Spirit, guide those who govern us, that they may be servants of the common good in Your name.
R. *Christ, hear us.*

Pour out Your Spirit, the protector of the poor, to help and lift up all those in need.
R. *Christ, hear us.*

We pray for all stewards of Your mysteries, that they may always be found faithful.
R. *Christ, hear us.*

By Your suffering, resurrection and ascension You accomplished our redemption; bring it to completion in the souls and bodies of the dead.
R. *Christ, hear us.*

Wednesday

In company with the apostles and all who have the first fruits of the Holy Spirit; let us praise God and say:
R. *Lord, hear our prayer.*

Almighty God, You raised Christ to glory in Heaven; may all mankind recognize His presence in the Church.
R. *Lord, hear our prayer.*

All-holy Father, You said of Christ: This is My beloved Son, hear Him; grant that all may hear His voice and be saved.
R. *Lord, hear our prayer.*

Send Your Spirit into the hearts of Your faithful people, as cleansing water and refreshing rain.
R. *Lord, hear our prayer.*

Send Your Spirit to guide the course of nature, and renew life over the face of the earth.
R. *Lord, hear our prayer.*

We commend to Your care all who have died, and ask You
to strengthen our hope in the resurrection to come.
R. *Lord, hear our prayer.*

Thursday

Christ is God, blessed for ever. Let us ask Him to send the
Holy Spirit on all redeemed by His Blood, as we say:
R. *Lord, look with favor on those You have redeemed.*

Send into the Church the Spirit of unity,
to remove all dissension, hatred and division.
R. *Lord, look with favor on those You have redeemed.*

You freed those possessed by devils;
free the world from the evils that afflict it.
R. *Lord, look with favor on those You have redeemed.*

You prayed, and were led by the Spirit to begin Your ministry; may priests find in prayer the guidance of the Spirit
to perform their duties.
R. *Lord, look with favor on those You have redeemed.*

May Your Spirit guide all in authority, to seek the common
good.
R. *Lord, look with favor on those You have redeemed.*

You live in the glory of the Father,
summon into Your glory all the departed.
R. *Lord, look with favor on those You have redeemed.*

Friday

Let us praise and thank the Father, Who has poured out the
grace of the Spirit on all peoples. Let us ask Him for an ever
greater share in His Spirit, saying:
R. *Lord pour out the grace of the Holy Spirit throughout the
world.*

Lord, You gave us Your chosen One as the light of all peoples; open the eyes of the blind, and lead from captivity those who sit in darkness.
R. *Lord pour out the grace of the Holy Spirit throughout the world.*

You anointed Christ by the power of the Holy Spirit for the ministry of salvation; may He once more go about the world, doing good and healing all.
R. *Lord pour out the grace of the Holy Spirit throughout the world.*

Send Your Spirit, the light of all hearts, to strengthen the faith of those in doubt.
R. *Lord pour out the grace of the Holy Spirit throughout the world.*

Send Your Spirit, our rest in labor, to support the weary and the broken-hearted.
R. *Lord pour out the grace of the Holy Spirit throughout the world.*

Fulfill the hope of those who have died, so that they may rise again at the coming of Christ.
R. *Lord pour out the grace of the Holy Spirit throughout the world.*

Saturday

When the days of Pentecost were complete, God sent the Holy Spirit upon the apostles. As we celebrate this great feast with joy and faith, let us cry out:
R. *Send forth Your Spirit and make the whole world new.*

In the beginning You created Heaven and earth, and in the fullness of time You renewed all things in Christ; through Your Spirit go on renewing the world with the gift of salvation.
R. *Send forth Your Spirit and make the whole world new.*

You breathed the breath of life into Adam; send Your Spirit into Your Church to be its life and vigor, that it may bring new life to the whole world.
R. *Send forth Your Spirit and make the whole world new.*

By the light of Your Spirit, enlighten the world and dispel the darkness of our times; turn hatred into love, sorrow into joy and war into the peace we so desire.
R. *Send forth Your Spirit and make the whole world new.*

Water flowed from the side of Christ as the fountain of Your Spirit; may it flow over all the earth and bring forth goodness.
R. *Send forth Your Spirit and make the whole world new.*

You bring life and glory to mankind through the Holy Spirit; through the Spirit lead the departed into the love and joy of Heaven.
R. *Send forth Your Spirit and make the whole world new.*

Pentecost

God the Father has gathered His Church in unity through Christ. With joy in our hearts let us ask Him:
R. *Send Your Holy Spirit into the Church.*

You desire the unity of all Christians through one baptism in the Spirit; make all who believe one in heart and soul.
R. *Send Your Holy Spirit into the Church.*

**You desire the whole world to be filled with the Spirit;
help all mankind to build a world of justice and peace.**
R. *Send Your Holy Spirit into the Church.*

**Lord God, Father of all mankind, You desire to gather
together Your scattered children in unity of faith; enlighten
the world
by the grace of the Holy Spirit.**
R. *Send Your Holy Spirit into the Church.*

**Through the Spirit You make all things new;
heal the sick, comfort the distressed, give salvation to all.**
R. *Send Your Holy Spirit into the Church.*

**Through the Spirit You raised Your Son from the dead;
raise up the bodies of the dead into everlasting life.**
R. *Send Your Holy Spirit into the Church.*

Litany of Peace

(Byzantine Divine Liturgy of St. John Chrysostom)

Priest: In peace let us pray to the Lord.
Response to each invocation: *Lord, have mercy.*

**Priest: For peace from on high and the salvation of souls,
let us pray to the Lord.**

**Priest: For peace in the whole world, the well-being of the
holy churches of God and for the union of all, let us
pray to the Lord.**

**Priest: For this holy place and for those who enter it with
faith, reverence and fear of God, let us pray to the
Lord.**

Priest: For our Bishop N . . . , the reverend priests, the deacons in Christ and for all the clergy and the people,
let us pray to the Lord.

Priest: For our public servants, for the government and for
all those who protect us, that they may be upheld and
strengthened in every good deed, let us pray to the
Lord.

Priest: For this city, for every city and country place, and
the faithful dwelling in them, let us pray to the Lord.

Priest: For favorable weather, an abundance of the fruits of
the earth and for peaceful times, let us pray to the
Lord.

Priest: For travelers by sea, air and land, for the sick and
the suffering, for those in prison, and for their salvation, let us pray to the Lord.

Priest: For our deliverance from all affliction, wrath, danger and need, let us pray to the Lord.

Priest: Help us, save us, have mercy on us, and protect us, O
God, by Your grace.

Priest: Let us remember our all-holy, spotless, most highly
blessed and glorious Lady, the Mother of God, and
ever-virgin Mary, with all the saints and commend
ourselves and one another, and our whole life to
Christ God.

All: *To You, O Lord.*

Priest: For all glory, honor and worship are Your due,
Father, Son and Holy Spirit, now and always and for
ever and ever.

All: *Amen.*

Ecumenic Prayer

(Byzantine Divine Liturgy of St. John Chrysostom)

Let us all say, with our whole soul and our whole mind, let us all say:
R. *Lord, have mercy.*

Lord Almighty, God of our fathers, we pray to You, hear us and have mercy.
R. *Lord, have mercy.*

Have mercy on us, O God, in Your great mercy: we pray to You, hear us and have mercy.
Response to the following invocations: *Lord, have mercy. Lord, have mercy. Lord, have mercy.*

Again, we pray for (His Beatitude our Patriarch N.,) our Most Reverend Bishop N., and for their reverend clergy.

Again, we pray for our brothers the priests, the monks, the deacons, and for all our brothers in Christ.

Again, we pray for mercy, life, peace, health, salvation, protection, forgiveness and remission of sins for the servants of God who live in this city (or village, or for the brethren of this holy monastery).

Again, we pray for the blessed and ever to be remembered founders of this holy church (or monastery), and for our Orthodox Fathers and brethren who have gone before us and who here or elsewhere have been laid to pious rest.

Again, we pray for those who bear offerings, those who do good works in this holy and most venerable church, those who toil, those who sing and all the people here present who await from You great and abundant mercy.

Priest: Again and many times we fall down before You and pray You in Your goodness and love for mankind to regard our supplications and cleanse our souls and bodies from all defilement of flesh and spirit, and grant that we may stand without guilt or condemnation before Your holy altar. And upon these also who pray with us, O God, bestow increase of life and faith and spiritual insight. Give them ever to minister to You in fear and love, to share without guilt or condemnation in Your holy mysteries and to be made worthy of Your heavenly kingdom. That being ever protected by Your power, we may send up glory to You, to the Father and the Son and the Holy Spirit, now and always and for ever and ever.

All: *Amen.*

Faith Publishing Company

Faith Publishing Company has been organized as a service for the publishing and distribution of materials that reflect Christian values, and in particular the teachings of the Catholic Church.

It is dedicated to publication of only those materials that reflect such values.

Faith Publishing Company also publishes books for The Riehle Foundation. The Foundation is a non-profit, tax-exempt producer and distributor of Catholic books and materials worldwide, and also supplies hospital and prison ministries, churches and mission organizations.

For more information on the publications of Faith Publishing Company, contact:

Faith Publishing Company
P.O. BOX 237
MILFORD, OHIO 45150

OTHER BOOKS
by Fr. George Kosicki, C.S.B.

SPIRITUAL WARFARE

Belief in the existence of Satan and evil spirits have been largely rejected in our age. Some straight-forward facts about the devil and his all-out warfare against God's people and how we can fight back.

146 pages   ISBN: 0-9625975-4-6   **$5.00**

LIVING EUCHARIST

Describes the transforming power of the three dimensions of the Eucharist. An answer to the crisis within the Church today.

60 pages   ISBN: 0-9625975-9-7   **$4.00**

ICONS OF MERCY

These letters on the mystery of mercy and Mary provide great insight to the needs, pressures, trials, and opportunities associated with the current state of the Church and the ordained ministry.

164 pages   ISBN: 0-9625975-0-3   **$6.00**

Books published by
Faith Publishing Company
can be ordered as follows:

Individuals send
requests to: The Riehle Foundation
P.O. Box 7
Milford, Ohio 45150
513-576-0032

Book stores and
centers, contact: Faith Publishing Company
P.O. Box 237
Milford, Ohio 45150
513-576-6400
513-576-0022 (Fax)

Canadian
Distributor: B. Broughton Company Limited
2105 Danforth Ave.
Toronto, Ontario
Canada M4C 1K1
416-690-4777
416-690-5357 (Fax)

About the author . . .

Father George W. Kosicki, C.S.B. was ordained in 1954. Sixteen years into his priesthood, he began to pursue his growing interest in spiritual renewal, prayer life, and experimental community life. He became actively involved in the Charismatic Renewal and with Houses of Prayer in the Detroit, Michigan area. From 1975 to 1983 he was coordinator of Bethany House of Intercession, a community of priests, bishops, and deacons. From 1983 to 1986 he was a member of the Fraternity of Priests associated with the Franciscan University of Steubenville, Ohio.

Led by a desire to promote the message of God's mercy that had been planted when his family was introduced to the Divine Mercy devotion in the 1940's, Father George spent two years with the Marians of Eden Hill in Stockbridge, Massachusetts. There he worked in the publishing headquarters of the Association of Marian Helpers, a full-time apostolate of writing, preaching, and publishing on the message of Divine Mercy. He has published a number of articles, books, and audio and video tapes. He is also in demand as a speaker at religious conferences and has made a number of television appearances, notably on EWTN.

Father Kosicki is currently at the Marian Helpers Center, Stockbridge, administering Divine Mercy International, an organization focused on trust in the mercy of God.